CHICAGO

AMERICA'S BEST SPORTS TOWN

BRIAN SANDALOW

FOREWORD BY
MIKE DITKA

First Edition
First Printing, 2018

Book design by Jake Slavik
Cover design by Jake Slavik
Photographs ©: Mark J. Terrill/AP Images, cover (top left), 95; Jim Biever/AP Images, cover (top middle left), 18; AP Images, cover (top middle right), cover (bottom middle left), back cover (top middle left), 36, 68–69, 105, 140–141, 159; Nam Y. Huh/AP Images, cover (top right), back cover (top middle right), 32–33, 133; Ian Johnson/Icon Sportswire/AP Images, cover (bottom left), 77; Tom DiPace/AP Images, cover (bottom middle right), 11; Charles Knoblock/AP Images, cover (bottom right), 24; marchello74/Shutterstock Images, cover (center); Mike Wulf/Cal Sport Media/AP Images, back cover (top left), 3, 42; Pro Football Hall of Fame/AP Images, back cover (top right), 116; Focus on Sport/Getty Images Sport/Getty Images, 5, 123; Ezra Shaw/Getty Images Sport/Getty Images, 6–7; Jonathan Daniel/Getty Images Sport/Getty Images, 9, 17, 22, 25, 60, 63, 75, 106–107; Scott Olson/Getty Images Sport/Getty Images, 13, 120; Christian Petersen/Getty Images Sport/Getty Images, 14–15; Andy Hayt/Sports Illustrated/Getty Images, 20; Dilip Vishwanat/Getty Images Sport/Getty Images, 26, 79; Focus on Sport/Getty Images, 28, 31, 47, 162 (top left), 168–169; Bettmann/Getty Images, 35, 129, 155; Dave Sandford/National Hockey League/Getty Images, 39; David E. Klutho/Sports Illustrated/Getty Images, 44, 153; Gregg Forwerck/National Hockey League/Getty Images, 48–49; Jeff Haynes/AFP/Getty Images, 50–51, 56; John Zich/AFP/Getty Images, 53; Manny Millan/Sports Illustrated/Getty Images, 58; Mitchell Layton/Getty Images Sport/Getty Images, 65; Doug Pensinger/Getty Images Sport/Getty Images, 67; Chris McGrath/Getty Images Sport/Getty Images, 71; Rich Pilling/MLB Photos/Getty Images Sport/Getty Images, 73; Raymond Boyd/Michael Ochs Archives/Getty Images, 74; Otto Greule Jr./Getty Images Sport/Getty Images, 83; John F. Jaqua/Sports Illustrated/Getty Images, 85, 162 (top right), 166–167; Ron Vesely/MLB Photos/Getty Images Sport/Getty Images, 86–87, 103; George Rinhart/Corbis Historical/Getty Images, 89; Sporting News/Sporting News/Getty Images, 91; G. N. Lowrance/Getty Images Sport/Getty Images, 92; Eugene Garcia/AFP/Getty Images, 96; Diamond Images/Getty Images, 101; NCAA Photos/Getty Images, 109; Zach Bolinger/Icon Sportswire/Getty Images, 111; Joe Robbins/Getty Images Sport/Getty Images, 113; Chicago History Museum/Archive Photos/Getty Images, 114, 157; Bruce Bennett Studios/Bruce Bennett/Getty Images, 118–119; Helmut Gritscher/Sports Illustrated/Getty Images, 121; David J. Phillip/AP Images, 125; Jasper Juinen/Getty Images Sport/Getty Images, 126; Matthew Ashton/EMPICS/PA Images/Getty Images, 130–131; Shaun Botterill/Getty Images Sport/Getty Images, 136; Mike Ehrmann/Getty Images Sport/Getty Images, 139; Keith Beaty/Toronto Star/Getty Images, 143; Nate Fine/Getty Images Sport/Getty Images, 144; Robert Riger/Getty Images Sport/Getty Images, 146; Dylan Buell/Getty Images Sport/Getty Images, 148–149; Jon Durr/Eclipse Sportswire/Getty Images Sport/Getty Images, 150; Mark McMahon/Corbis Historical/Getty Images, 151; Pigi Cipelli/Archivio Pigi Cipelli/Mondadori Portfolio/Getty Images, 152; Mark Rucker/Transcendental Graphics/Getty Images Sport/Getty Images, 154; Illinois/Collegiate Images/Getty Images, 161; MLB Photos/Hulton Archive/Getty Images, 162 (bottom left), 164–165; Owen C. Shaw/Getty Images Sport/Getty Images, 162 (bottom right), 170–171

Design Elements ©: Shutterstock Images

Press Box Books, an imprint of Press Room Editions, Inc.

Library of Congress Cataloging-in-Publication Data
978-1-63494-029-0

Distributed by North Star Editions, Inc.
2297 Waters Drive
Mendota Heights, MN 55120
www.northstareditions.com

Printed in the United States of America

TABLE OF CONTENTS

I love Chicago.

I love the Bears. I love the Blackhawks. I love the Bulls. The White Sox and the Cubs. I love them all. I'm a Chicago fan. I'm a Chicago person. Yeah, I spend half of my time at my home in Naples, Florida, but the rest of the time I'm here overseeing my four restaurants. But more important, Chicago is my kind of town.

It has been that way since I arrived in 1961, though I didn't really know what I was doing when I first showed up. My then-wife Marge was pregnant, and I had just signed a contract with the Bears. We ended up getting an apartment on the North Side before moving out to the suburbs. Quickly, though, something became apparent: Chicago is a great sports town, and I've seen that firsthand.

The run I had with the Bears began in 1961. We had a lot of good players and great coaches, and we won it all in 1963. Then, during training camp before the 1964 season, Willie Galimore and Bo Farrington died in an automobile accident, and that took us down. In 1965, we added Dick Butkus and Gale Sayers and had maybe the best team in the NFL, but we fell short in the Western Conference.

My career with the Bears was terrific, but when George Halas got sick of my act, they shipped me off to Philadelphia. That didn't last. Going to Dallas next changed my life because I met Tom Landry. Outside of my high school coach and my father and Halas, he was probably the most influential guy in my life.

Then, in 1982, I came back to coach the Bears. I felt like I was a better person; you learn from your mistakes. And by 1985, we were champions again. We had a great group of players, and we won the Super Bowl. But that wasn't all on me. I've been lucky to be put in great positions to succeed, and had a lot of great people around me and a lot of people who not only believed in me but believed in what we were trying to do, and we accomplished the ultimate goal.

You don't get anywhere in life without setting goals, and maybe I set mine too high sometimes. But if you're going to set goals, you might as well set them way up there. If you don't quite make it, you still might get something pretty good, and I really believe in that.

Another thing I believe in is that Chicago doesn't owe me anything. I owe my whole life to Chicago and the Bears. Anybody who doesn't understand that is crazy. I'm a Bears fan; I was a Bears fan. I will be a Bears fan forever. That's just the facts.

And though I'm a Western Pennsylvania guy, I've become a Chicago sports fan.

I think anybody who ever watched Michael Jordan play basketball became a fan of the Bulls. If you didn't, you had to be blind. I became a Blackhawks fan in the early 1960s when I was playing with the Bears. A friend of mine had Hawks season tickets and used to take me to games at Chicago Stadium. I love hockey, and I got to know Stan Mikita and Bobby Hull and Glenn Hall and the rest of the players.

▲ Bears players carry Ditka off the field following their win in Super Bowl XX.

Oh, as I mentioned, I love the Cubs. I love what Joe Maddon is doing. Not just the fact that they won a World Series but that they're doing the right things. They've got great young players who play hard and look like they're having fun. Joe brings that to them and has brought another championship to a city that deserves winners.

And yes, I love the White Sox, as well. That's one thing I don't understand about this city, that some North Siders don't like the White Sox and some South Siders don't love the Cubs.

Other than that, Chicago sports and the city as a whole make sense to me. My hometown, Pittsburgh, is a mini Chicago. The people work hard, and the city is a melting pot that comes together for its sports.

Los Angeles is a great sports town. New York is a great sports town. Philadelphia is a great sports town. But in Chicago, everybody who lives there has persevered for a lot of years through the good and bad. Together.

Mike Ditka was a Hall of Fame tight end for the Bears from 1961 to 1966 and coached the team from 1982 to 1992, winning the 1963 NFL title as a player and Super Bowl XX as a coach.

CHICAGO SPORTS TOWN

I t wasn't just a victory celebration. It wasn't just fans hitting the streets and hitting the bottles the night their team won a title. There was something more to the early morning of November 3, 2016, when the Cubs beat the Cleveland Indians to win their first World Series since 1908.

Yes, there were the usual signs of depravity and partying, but there was a different feeling on the Chicago streets. Religious might be too strong a word, but there was deliverance and the faithful receiving their reward for years and decades of belief. Happiness wasn't the lone emotion; it was joined by a cathartic relief that, finally, the wait had been worth it.

When people celebrated, they didn't just do it for themselves. They did it so they could remember whom they were with and, more poignant, who hadn't lived to see Kris Bryant throw to Anthony Rizzo to end the famous 108-year drought. This one was for the grandparents who couldn't quite

◀ Catcher David Ross became a folk hero for Cubs fans en route to the team's historic 2016 World Series title.

hold out long enough; the parents, relatives, and friends who were taken too soon; and the unborn kids who would have to check Facebook to see how Mom and Dad cried their eyes out when the celebration began.

Some fans marked the moment by scribbling something in chalk on the outfield walls at Wrigley Field. Others went to the graves of deceased Cubs fans, and all savored how they had seen something practically nobody alive could remember.

"She would have loved this," Angelica Velez said, according to the *Chicago Sun-Times*, at the grave of her grandmother Anna Romero, who died in 2009. "She was the biggest Cubs fan. I came here last week, when they made the (World Series) to tell her. I told her they were going to win, and they did."

The Cubs' 2016 triumph will go down in history as one of Chicago's great moments. But it's not the only great moment, and it's certainly not the only moment in which the faithful got what they deserved.

Chicago itself is home to five teams that are foundational members of their leagues. It's hard to envision pro football becoming much of anything without George Stanley Halas, who founded the Bears and was pivotal in the birth and development of the NFL. The Cubs were among the original members of the National League in 1876 and one of the circuit's first dynasties. The White Sox won the first American League pennant in 1901, and owner Charles Comiskey was one of the earliest titans of the AL. The Blackhawks are one of the NHL's Original Six and have as colorful a history as any team in hockey. And the "youngster" of the group, the Bulls, have left an indelible mark on Chicago, the NBA, and sports culture as a whole since their founding in 1966.

THEN AND ALWAYS Bears fans cheer as the team shuts out the Los Angeles Rams in the NFC Championship Game on January 12, 1986.

As a sports town, Chicago is built around its big five. Each of the five franchises has enjoyed at least one championship since 1985. But there is much more to the city than the five major teams. The city has been home to incredible high school basketball, supports local Big Ten teams Northwestern and Illinois (not to mention Notre Dame), and has the rare distinction of being home to champions of both Major League Soccer and the old North American Soccer League. There is also the Chicago Sky, which reached the WNBA Finals in 2014, and the Chicago Red Stars of the National Women's Soccer League.

The only thing missing from Chicago's sports resume is an Olympic Games, as the 1904 event was swiped by St. Louis, and the city shockingly lost its bid for 2016.

Michael Jordan, Walter Payton, Stan Mikita, Ernie Banks, and Frank Thomas are just a few of the names to have graced courts, fields, and arenas in the Windy City. Those stars and others were showered with applause in iconic venues such as Wrigley Field, Comiskey Park, Chicago Stadium, and Soldier Field, places that could send a shiver down your spine.

Perhaps most important, the fans of the big five teams know both heartbreak and the dedication to push ahead. Each of the five teams has put its fans through moments (and decades) where doubt would be a valid response, as would finding a new hobby.

Of course, the Cubs lead the pack in this department. Mention the 1969 New York Mets to fans of a certain vintage, and they'll cringe and curse what should have been a triumphant summer. Talk about Leon Durham and the 1984 San Diego Padres, and the conversation will turn cold—quickly. And as for 2003—just don't go there.

In the end, that hasn't stopped Cubs fans from being as dedicated as any fan base ever. Wrigley has drawn fans from all over the globe, some who come simply to visit a tourist attraction but also many who come to see their team and have the chance to say, "Yeah, I saw the team that did it."

White Sox fans don't get the same credit nationally, but theirs, too, is an unmistakable passion. They had to wait 88 years between World Series championships and, unlike their North Side rivals, didn't have the captivating stories to create a mystique. Tell a random national fan about Jerry Dybzinski's base-running gaffe in Game 4 of the 1983 American League Championship Series against Baltimore, and you'll get blank stares. But that's a part of the Sox story. And their fans wear that scar with pride.

The Bulls, of course, were blessed with Jordan, but even they had to wait. They endured year after year after year of heartbreak and disappointment in losing to the Pistons. But they finally broke through in 1991 and went on to become an iconic NBA dynasty, with millions of young kids around the globe wishing to be like Mike. Every championship was celebrated with a massive rally in Grant Park as fans bonded over their world-famous powerhouse. Even today, as memories of the dynasty fade further, the Bulls still lead the NBA in attendance and are a uniquely Chicago franchise representing the city in a sport it has mastered.

▲ Michael Jordan led the NBA in points per game in each of the 10 full seasons he played from 1986–87 to 1997–98.

The Blackhawks made their fans wait 49 years for a Stanley Cup but delivered three between 2010 and 2015. Derided by some as fair-weather, Hawks fans just needed a reason to support their team. Try getting a ticket to a game at the United Center. Good luck. Chicago fans went through as much as anybody but now treat their players like princes of the city. Jonathan Toews, Patrick Kane, Duncan Keith, and Brent Seabrook are rewards for a half century of disappointment, but the passion was always there.

Maybe the team that has put its fans through the least is the Bears, but don't accuse their fans of lacking passion. When the Bears are good, they are the toast of the town, the sun to the city's solar system, the oxygen everybody breathes. That's true even today, as their title drought is actually the longest in the city. If you had any doubts, check out how Bears fans turned out for the Super Bowl parade on January 27, 1986. After 22 years of waiting for a title, a wind chill of minus-32 wasn't going to stop 300,000 of them from celebrating.

In fact, according to the *Chicago Tribune*, organizers routed the parade on LaSalle Street, instead of down the wider Michigan Avenue, because they didn't expect such a huge crowd.

"LaSalle Street would have been fine for the crowd we were expecting," police First Deputy Superintendent John Jemilo said, according to the *Tribune*. "It was a workday, a school day, and it was cold. Had anyone suggested the crowd would be larger, we would have changed the route to something like Michigan Avenue, or maybe we would have stretched it out for a long distance along Dearborn."

Jemilo and the city shouldn't have been surprised. These were Chicago fans, people whose bond with their teams goes beyond wins and losses. It's about the identity of a metropolis in the middle of the country that adores its teams and connects with its players. Separated during the summer, Chicagoans come together to bleed for their teams and are willing to put up with the pain and disappointment for the ultimate reward.

That's why Chicago is America's Best Sports Town.

WHAT A VIEW Fans took whatever seats they could find in Grant Park to watch the Blackhawks' 2015 Stanley Cup championship parade.

CHAPTER 1

THE BEARS

There's just something different about Chicago's relationship with the Bears. When they're good, there's a different pulse in the area. The days between games take forever, and on Sundays everybody is united with a purpose to see the Monsters of the Midway win.

Since coming to Chicago in 1921, the Bears have treated their fans to glory and triumph. It began with George Halas as a player and coach, leading teams with the legendary Bronko Nagurski and Red Grange. In 1932, the latter two led the Bears to victory in the first NFL Championship Game, which was played indoors at Chicago Stadium, as Wrigley Field was frozen over. The 1940s had the Sid Luckman dynasty and 73–0; the 1960s had the 1963 champions of Mike Ditka, Ed O'Bradovich, and Doug Atkins; and then Dick Butkus and Gale Sayers followed as Wrigley Field became known as much for football as for baseball.

◀ Cornerback Charles Tillman celebrates en route to a pick six against the Arizona Cardinals in 2012.

The Bears finally moved to Soldier Field in 1971, but they soon made history by drafting Walter Payton and building toward the glorious 1980s, which were capped by coach Mike Ditka (Halas's last hire) and the Super Bowl XX champion shuffling crew that was boosted by Buddy Ryan's stifling 46 defense.

> "Some say the 46 is just an eight-man front. That's like saying Marilyn Monroe is just a girl."
> — **Buddy RYAN**
> BEARS DEFENSIVE COORDINATOR (1978–1985)

That set the stage for the next generation, with Brian Urlacher, Lance Briggs, and Lovie Smith bringing the Bears to the doorstep of another title in 2006, while Jay Cutler helped move the Bears' offense into the future with his strong arm.

Throughout their history, the Bears have been a reflection of their city. Tough but forward thinking, respectful of history but not paralyzed by the past. They moved from Wrigley to Soldier Field and then redid their stadium by the lake so they wouldn't have to rebuild again for decades. Their uniforms are essentially the same but tweaked enough so they're contemporary. They perfected the T formation and were the first team to use a middle linebacker.

The Bears are a team Chicagoans share. No parts of town cheer for different teams. Everywhere you go, it's all Bears. This is the Bears, a special part of Chicago.

The 1985 Bears

There's a common thought in Chicago that the shadow of the 1985 team will fade when the Bears finally win their second Super Bowl title.

Not a chance.

The '85 Bears will always be a part of Chicago sports culture, no matter how many championships the team wins.

No team will ever have the personalities of the '85 Bears. No "Samurai" Mike Singletary, no "Punky QB" Jim McMahon, no "Iron" Mike Ditka, no "Sweetness" Walter Payton, no Steve "Mongo" McMichael, no William "The Refrigerator" Perry. This was a special group of players who combined to do something that will never be matched. They weren't just football stars. They crossed into popular culture with "The Super Bowl Shuffle" and stayed there, as seemingly every player had commercials or radio shows. The fans were even lampooned on *Saturday Night Live* by the Super Fans.

These Bears—they were big.

"Like the Beatles, there was a Bear for every sort of fan," Rich Cohen wrote in *Monsters: The 1985 Chicago Bears and the Wild Heart of Football*.

Oh, they were also good. Dominant. Historically good. That helps.

SWEETNESS Walter Payton led the Bears to a 45–10 win over Washington on September 29, 1985.

Entering the 1985 season, the Bears were expected to do great things. Coming off a loss to the San Francisco 49ers in the NFC Championship Game, the 1985 Bears were favored to go one step further and give the franchise its first title since 1963. The season started with wins over Tampa Bay, New England, Minnesota, Washington, and Tampa Bay again. At 5–0, the Bears went back to the Bay to face a 49ers team that had humiliated them in the playoffs the previous year, using guard Guy McIntyre as a fullback to rub it in. Ditka remembered and countered by using Perry out of the backfield for the first time. The next week, Perry scored against Green Bay on *Monday Night Football*, and the Bears were on track to emerge as the greatest team of all time. "They will write songs about William Perry," announcer Frank Gifford gushed during the win over Green Bay.

One song in particular was coming about Perry and his teammates: "The Super Bowl Shuffle." And in the absolute height of hubris, it was recorded the day after the Bears suffered their only loss of the season, a humbling 38–24 defeat on *Monday Night Football* to the Dolphins, who saved the legacy of their 1972 team as the only unbeaten squad in league history.

"The timing was impeccable," backup quarterback Mike Tomczak said, according to *Slate.* "Somebody had a watch on us, whether it was Papa Bear Halas or somebody else who had a beacon over us. When this came to fruition, not only did we help out a lot of families through the charity dollars, but we gained national exposure. With the addition of MTV and all the video outlets, that song was playing constantly in the Chicago market once it was released, and we fulfilled the prophecy of winning a Super Bowl and sold more than one million copies."

Not only did the Bears win the Super Bowl; they did it in a dominant fashion rarely seen before or since. They went 15–1 in the regular season and swept through the postseason, becoming the second team in league history to go 18–1 overall. They won five regular-season games by 20 points or more and had the best defense and offense in the NFC.

In the playoffs, they punished the Giants 21–0 and then blanked the Rams 24–0 to enter the Super Bowl as heavy favorites over New England. Bears fans practically invaded New Orleans for the big game, as their team was the main attraction. McMahon mooned a news helicopter, and the Bears saw the French Quarter as much as they saw their hotel rooms.

HIGH FIVE Otis Wilson (55) and William "The Refrigerator" Perry celebrate the Bears' win in Super Bowl XX.

But none of that mattered. The Bears battered the overwhelmed Patriots 46–10 to complete the most dominant playoff run in NFL history. The Bears had offensive touchdowns, a defensive score, a safety, and even a touchdown from Perry, as they staked their claim to history and cemented their place in league history. Other than Payton not scoring a touchdown and a career-ending knee injury to defensive back Leslie Frazier, January 26, 1986, will go down as a perfect day in Chicago history, when a group of men became civic legends. To cap things off, Ditka and defensive coordinator Buddy Ryan—who had feuded during their time together—were both carried off the field by the players.

But that was it for championships for the 1980s Bears. Ryan left for Philadelphia, and injuries, attrition, and upsets kept the Bears from winning more.

Maybe that's why memories of the 1985 team endure.

THE FIVE GREATEST PLAYS IN
BEARS HISTORY

5. Mike Brown Does It Twice (October 28, 2001, and November 4, 2001)

Nobody expected much of the 2001 Bears after a poor 2000 season, but they had luck on their side. Brown exemplified that, returning deflected interceptions for game-winning overtime touchdowns in consecutive weeks to beat the 49ers and Browns.

4. Devin Hester's Super Start (February 4, 2007)

The Colts kicked to Devin Hester to start Super Bowl XLI, and the rookie made Indianapolis pay. After receiving the ball on the left side of the field, Hester worked through the middle, broke free, and was taken down only as he crossed the goal line for a 92-yard score. Unfortunately for the Bears, that was their high-water mark, as they lost 29–17.

3. A Block Sets the Tone (December 8, 1940)

The 1940 NFL Championship Game was a historic rout, as the Bears crushed Washington 73–0. The tone was set on the second play of the game when Bill Osmanski bounced outside and streaked down the left sideline for a 68-yard touchdown. Though the run was impressive, the play lives on because of George Wilson's block that leveled two Washington defenders and gave Osmanski an open route to the end zone.

2. Ditka's Dash (November 24, 1963)

Heartbroken over the assassination of President John F. Kennedy two days earlier, the Bears traveled to Pittsburgh. Trailing 17–14 in the fourth quarter, the Bears needed a score to keep pace with Green Bay for the Western Conference lead. Quarterback Bill Wade threw to Mike Ditka, who broke six tackles and rambled 63 yards to get the Bears into position for the game-tying field goal.

1. On to Super Bowl XX (January 12, 1986)

Leading the 1985 NFC Championship Game 17–0, the Bears were minutes from the Super Bowl, but the Rams had the ball near midfield. As the snow began to fall at Soldier Field, Rams quarterback Dieter Brock was hit and stripped by Richard Dent. Wilber Marshall picked up the fumble and returned it 52 yards for a touchdown. Bears fans had the chills, but not because of the weather.

A Legacy of Defense

Even if you didn't know the first thing about football, you would think of toughness when you heard the name *Chicago Bears*. Anything with a moniker that combines the great Midwestern metropolis and one of the fiercest creatures on the planet has to be mean and ferocious.

That's what the Bears have tried to be throughout their history. Especially on defense.

"In Chicago, you can always rely on defense. And we love defense," *Chicago Sun-Times* columnist Rick Telander said on an NFL Films production. "The simple fact is, we like the brutality of football. We like players saying, 'I'm not just going to tackle that guy. I'm going to kill him.' There's a part of us that says: 'We've got winter coming; we've got blizzards on the way. Lake Michigan is frozen solid. Well, how about we inflict a little pain on people who come here to visit?'"

The Bears have been doing that since moving to Chicago in 1921. Their greatest teams have all had that defensive blood in common. The 1930s and 1940s teams that made up the first NFL dynasty were filled with two-way players who shined on both sides of the ball. Sid Luckman was a star quarterback and defensive back, Clyde "Bulldog" Turner was strong on both lines, and Ed Sprinkle caught seven touchdown passes while also starring as an elite pass rusher before the sack became an official statistic.

The Bears weren't as successful during the 1950s, but that's when the reputation for tough defenses truly became part of their DNA. George Halas was molding his teams to be like him: cranky, vicious, and really stingy.

In 1952, the team drafted linebacker Bill George from Wake Forest. He is credited with being the first great middle linebacker and, depending on whom you ask, the first middle linebacker. Period. Doug Atkins was acquired in 1955, and slowly but surely the pieces were getting put into place. By the 1963 season, the Bears' defense had Atkins, George, Stan Jones, Ed O'Bradovich, Richie Petitbon, and a cast of characters that was not looking to be friendly.

"Hell or high water, the Bears were going to put a physical beating on you," Bears defensive back Dave Whitsell said in an NFL Films production. "I don't care whether you won or lost, you were going to know you were in the damnedest game you ever been in in your whole life."

The Giants would agree, losing 14–10 to the Bears in the 1963 NFL Championship Game. That day at a frigid Wrigley Field was the perfect microcosm of the season. The offense did just enough and the defense dominated, giving Halas the last of his six championships as coach.

But that wasn't Halas's last great group on defense. Two years later, Dick Butkus was the third overall pick in the draft and became the single most feared person in NFL history. His hits were the stuff of legend, and he still sets the standard for linebackers. He made NFL players, not usually the scaring type, frightened. They knew he was coming and would brace themselves for impact, while coaches had to game-plan around him.

WINNERS Coach George Halas, linebacker Bill George (61), and defensive back Larry Glueck (43) celebrate a 1963 Bears win over the Packers in Green Bay.

"The plan was to not run between the tackles: always ensure that you block Dick," San Francisco 49ers guard Howard Mudd said. "Once the game started, the plan changed, though. It became, 'Don't run. Just pass.'"

Butkus's career ended after the 1973 season when his bad knees finally caught up with him. That wasn't the end of the Bears' legacy of defense, though. Instead, it was carried on through the 1970s and into the '80s when a new group, led by defensive coordinator Buddy Ryan, terrorized the NFL with their 46 defense. With Ryan, the 1985 Bears won Super Bowl XX 46–10, and the next year—after Ryan had left to coach Philadelphia— the Bears' defense was even better, setting a record for fewest points allowed in a 16-game season, a mark that stood until the 2000 Ravens broke it.

That crew—with Mike Singletary, Dave Duerson, Gary Fencik, Dan Hampton, Steve McMichael, Wilber Marshall, and the rest—would have made Halas proud. Their goal was to inflict pain and win.

Unfortunately for the Bears, they weren't able to maintain that tradition through the 1990s. But it came back in a big way in 2000 when they picked a kid from New Mexico with the ninth overall draft pick. Right away, it was obvious that Brian Urlacher was the heir the Bears and their fans were looking for.

▲ Brian Urlacher's 1,040 tackles rank as the most in Bears history.

' That's the best part of being a linebacker in Chicago," Urlacher said, according to ChicagoBears.com. "All you ever hear about is Singletary and Butkus and how good they were. It's a dream come true. Hopefully, I can carry on the tradition."

Urlacher did more than that. Under the guidance of defense-first Lovie Smith, Urlacher, Lance Briggs, Charles Tillman, Tommie Harris, and the Bears continued the tradition of defense. The 2006 team reached Super Bowl XLI and lost to the Colts, but those players still won their place in team history.

The Rivalry: Green Bay Packers

When Lovie Smith was hired in 2004 to replace Dick Jauron, he had no connection to the Bears. He was meant to bring a fresh start after a disappointing 2003 season. But Smith was smart enough to know how to win over fans quickly.

"The No. 1 goal that we'll have, the No. 1 goal, is to beat Green Bay," Smith told the media at his introductory news conference. "I feel the pain of seven years that the Chicago fans have of losing to them. I've been on the winning side the last five times I've played them, so I think we know how to beat them."

Those words were soothing to Bears fans, who had been tortured over the previous decade by Brett Favre, and a savvy move by Smith to get Chicago on his side. He recognized that Bears-Packers is the oldest rivalry in the NFL, dating back to the league's second season in 1921, and the closest, with the teams even at 94–94–6 entering the 2017 season. The characters are colorful, the coaches are legendary, and the games have an extra juice even if one of the teams is out of contention.

There's simply nothing like the Bears-Packers rivalry, and Smith picked up on that

The Packers have figured in some of the Bears' greatest moments. There was the poignant 14–13 win over Green Bay in 1999, when Bryan Robinson blocked a short Ryan Longwell kick to deliver a win in the Bears' first game after Walter Payton's death. William Perry became a national celebrity when he scored a touchdown against Green Bay on

Monday Night Football in 1985, and he caught a game-winning touchdown pass later that season at Lambeau Field.

The Packers have also delivered pain. In 1986, Charles Martin's dirty takedown of Jim McMahon ended the QB's season and was an early blow to the Bears' hopes of repeating as Super Bowl champions. In 1989, Don Majkowski and instant replay beat the Bears when Majkowski was ruled not to have been over the line of scrimmage for his game-winning touchdown pass. The 1990s brought Favre's dominance, but the 2010 NFC Championship Game was the ultimate disappointment for Chicago when Aaron Rodgers beat the Bears as an injured Jay Cutler watched from the Soldier Field sideline. Then, in 2013, a Rodgers bomb to Randall Cobb in Week 17 at Chicago gave the Packers a division title and ended the Bears' season.

The teams have been measuring sticks for each other, each always looking to spoil seasons and eras for the other. As you would expect, that leads to hatred between each team's fans. Bears fans always make fun of Green Bay and Wisconsin as a whole, while Packers fans mock the Bears' traditions.

It's a wholly unique rivalry that's defined by great teams, great stadiums, some of the game's greatest players, and the fans.

"The two franchises have combined to win 21 world championships. But most of all, the fans are what make Packers-Bears the rivalry that it is," wrote Wayne Larrivee, the Green Bay radio announcer who jumped from the Bears in 1999. "Your passion reverberates all the way to the line of scrimmage."

Smith got that.

CHICAGO BEARS
MOUNT RUSHMORE

Dick Butkus (1965–1973)

What do you think of when you think of the Bears? A grunting, snarling, ferocious linebacker looking to destroy the opponent carrying the ball?

If so, you're thinking of Butkus.

No man was born more for his job than Butkus. A native of Chicago's South Side and an alum of the University of Illinois, Butkus came to the Bears in the same draft as Gale Sayers. For nine seasons before his career was cut short because of knee problems, Butkus was unquestionably the meanest and fiercest player in the NFL, and his legacy lives on today as a symbol of toughness and guts.

Beyond his hard-hitting and generally mean demeanor on the field, Butkus was one of the NFL's most athletic players during the 1960s and 1970s. He played on special teams and even caught a game-winning extra point, and he had good enough hands to intercept 22 passes.

Mike Ditka (1961–1966, player, 1982–1992, coach)

Simply put, few men have influenced an organization the way Ditka influenced the Bears. On the field, Ditka changed how the tight end can affect offenses. Before his arrival in 1961, NFL tight ends were basically expected to block and, in effect, be the sixth offensive lineman. Ditka changed that with his athleticism and great hands. He was such a great player that in 1988 he was the first tight end inducted into the Hall of Fame.

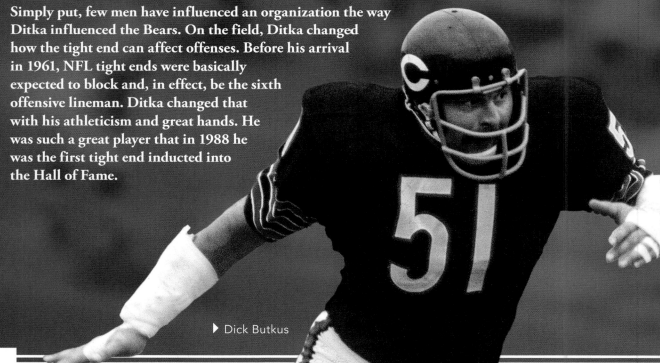

▶ Dick Butkus

After playing stints with Philadelphia and Dallas and time spent as an assistant coach with the Cowboys, Ditka returned to the Bears in 1982 as Halas's final head-coaching hire. That hire was a good one, as Ditka willed the Bears to greatness in the 1980s and the Super Bowl XX victory over New England. And though Ditka was fired after the 1992 season, he is still a Chicago icon who defined two generations of Bears football. That's hard to top.

George Halas (1920–1983)

There would be no Chicago Bears without George Stanley Halas. And there might not be an NFL, either. For more than six decades, Halas was the Bears. He helped cofound the NFL, spent time as a star Bears player, and coached the team to six of its NFL championships. He was also the only owner the Bears knew until his passing in 1983.

As a coach and owner, Halas built the Bears into the NFL's first dynasty, moving them from tiny Decatur, Illinois, to Chicago in 1921 and beginning the growth of the sport into America's favorite game. He helped perfect the T formation, which was football's first modern offense, and became the first coach to win 300 games.

Everything about the modern-day Bears still traces back to Halas. They wear the burnt orange and navy blue he chose to emulate the University of Illinois, his alma mater. They carry the name he chose to emulate the Cubs, and their left sleeve is adorned with his GSH initials and will be for as long as his influence on the team is felt.

Which will be forever.

Walter Payton (1975–1987)

Payton was not just the greatest running back but the greatest all-around football player of all time. To reel off his statistical accomplishments doesn't do his game justice, even though he retired as the NFL's leading rusher with 16,726 yards and as a nine-time Pro Bowler who starred for the 1985 Super Bowl champions.

He was a willing blocker and excellent pass-catcher, and he even knew how to throw a pass when his opportunity came. There was no player—offensive or defensive, skill player or lineman—who excelled in all facets of the game like "Sweetness," who had to wait until the end of his career to play for a true contender.

He didn't run away from contact or look to get out of bounds at the first chance. Payton wanted contact and usually came away the victor, thanks to his work ethic and well-known workouts that saw him run up hills in the middle of sticky Chicago summers.

Payton was a remarkable physical specimen who missed just one game during his 13-year career. And that made his death, in 1999 at age 45 from a rare liver disease, even more stunning and heartbreaking.

CHICAGO BEARS
BEST OF THE REST

Doug Atkins (1955–1966)

Atkins was an eight-time Pro Bowl selection, a member of the NFL's all-1960s team, and, most important, a standout defensive end on the Bears' 1963 championship team. He used his athleticism to break up passes and, if sacks were an official stat during his career, he surely would be among the all-time leaders.

Red Grange (1925, 1929–1934)

Grange's numbers as a halfback weren't great and his pro career was hobbled by a serious knee injury, but the Galloping Ghost was one of the NFL's first celebrities and a big reason why the nascent league gained a foothold in the 1920s and 1930s.

Dan Hampton (1979–1990)

"Danimal" was a star defensive end and defensive tackle for the Bears during their 1980s heyday and could have been even better if not for five surgeries on each knee and injuries that forced him to miss 23 games.

Sid Luckman (1939–1950)

Luckman remains the greatest quarterback in Bears history thanks to his four NFL championships and a mess of other league awards and honors. Arguably, the Bears haven't been the same since his retirement. Jay Cutler might have eclipsed him statistically, but there's no argument as to who was the better player.

Bronko Nagurski (1930–1937, 1943)

In the annals of tough Bears, maybe nobody stands out like Nagurski. At 6'2" and more than 220 pounds, Nagurski was a giant for his era. The University of Minnesota product was a terror to tackle as a fullback and a handful for opposing offenses to handle as a defensive lineman. Retired for five seasons and with the Bears shorthanded due to World War II, Nagurski came back and helped lead the team to the 1943 NFL championship.

Gale Sayers (1965–1971)

He played only 68 games in the NFL, but Sayers's 68 games were among the most breathtaking by a running back in NFL history, filled with dazzling moves and defenders left helpless in his wake. After a catastrophic knee injury in 1968, Sayers recovered to gain 1,032 yards the next season despite losing his trademark elusiveness. It might be his greatest accomplishment. Even more than Mark Prior or Derrick Rose, Sayers stands out as the greatest and most painful "what if?" in Chicago sports history.

Mike Singletary (1981–1992)

The owner of the scariest eyes in NFL history, Singletary was the leader of the famous 1985 Bears defense and was also named to 10 Pro Bowls and won a pair of Defensive Player of the Year honors (1985, 1988). "Samurai" called the defensive signals for the Super Bowl champions and will go down in history as one of the franchise's smartest players.

Clyde "Bulldog" Turner (1940–1952)

A seven-time All-Pro, Turner was a star center and defensive back and a part of four NFL championship teams during the 1940s dynasty. George Halas lauded his intelligence and apparently thought highly of his stamina, rarely taking him off the field.

Brian Urlacher (2000–2012)

Drafted in 2000, Urlacher is the latest to uphold the Bears' tradition of great middle linebackers. He was the 2005 Defensive Player of the Year and the heart and soul of the 2006 NFC champions. When he was unceremoniously dumped before the 2013 season, something about the Bears franchise fundamentally changed. In 2018, he followed Bill George, Dick Butkus, and Singletary as Bears linebackers elected to the Hall of Fame.

▶ Gale Sayers

CHAPTER 2
THE BLACKHAWKS

Before every game at the United Center, the Blackhawks play a series of videos on the center-ice scoreboard. There's the typical tribute to Chicago and the dramatic one that ends with the Hawks hitting the ice. One video that was inexplicably dropped for the 2017–18 season wasn't as loud or exciting, but it explained why 21,000 people lose their minds every time the home team scores.

Complemented by audio of legendary announcer Lloyd Pettit and current voices-of-the-team Pat Foley and John Wiedeman, classic highlights were shown: Bobby Hull and Stan Mikita in their prime, Jeremy Roenick sprinting down the ice, and Tony Esposito making saves—all with an image of the Blackhawks logo spliced into the highlights. At the end, all the great names in franchise history were listed, wrapping up with owner Rocky Wirtz.

◀ The arrival of Jonathan Toews in 2007–08 helped turn the Blackhawks into the NHL's most envied team.

In just three minutes, one video highlighted why the Blackhawks are a special part of Chicago. This Original Six franchise has been graced by some of hockey's greatest players, most colorful personalities, and iconic teams. Since their birth in 1926, the Hawks have become an integral part of Chicago. They've won six Stanley Cup titles and blessed the city with some of its greatest sports moments: the two goals in 17 seconds and the modern-day dynasty, the electric 1980s, the oh-so-close '90s, the era of steady greatness in the 1960s and early '70s, and even the two forgotten Stanley Cups in 1934 and 1938.

> "The noise and the excitement that comes from the anthem at United Center is unbelievable. There's not a guy in this room that won't tell you he gets the chills when he hears the place roar."
>
> - Adam *BURISH*
> BLACKHAWKS RIGHT WING, IN 2010

It's the cheering through "The Star-Spangled Banner," "Chelsea Dagger" driving opposing goalies nuts, and the beautiful red, white, and black jerseys. It's the roar of Chicago Stadium and the din of the new United Center. It's title rallies with hundreds of thousands of people and a city needing just a hint of a reason to love its team. It's three goals in 21 seconds by Bill Mosienko. It's Stan Mikita and Bobby Hull inventing the curved stick.

These are the Blackhawks, a unique part of Chicago.

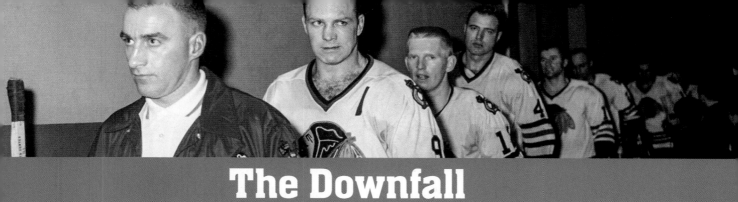

The Downfall

In 1966, the Blackhawks were in the middle of a golden era. Bobby Hull and Stan Mikita were two of the NHL's best forwards. Pierre Pilote was the game's best defenseman, and goalie Glenn Hall was in the middle of a Hall of Fame career. Five years earlier, the Blackhawks had won the Stanley Cup, their first title in 23 years.

It was a good time to be in the family business, and in 1966 William W. Wirtz, the son of owner Arthur Wirtz, rose to become the team's president.

With his father still around, Bill Wirtz didn't change much. And, frankly, there was no reason to mess with anything in the late 1960s. The Hawks were winners, filling Chicago Stadium as the unquestioned top winter draw in the city. Though the Hawks never could reclaim the Cup, including a devastating loss in the 1971 Stanley Cup Final to Montreal, there was little reason to believe they would fall from their perch.

Then the summer of 1972 hit, and everything changed.

The upstart World Hockey Association needed a star, and the Winnipeg Jets focused on getting just that in Hull. Bad blood had already been brewing between the Wirtzes and Hull, and the situation boiled over when the Jets and WHA offered the conveniently nicknamed Golden Jet a 10-year, $1.75 million deal plus a $1 million signing bonus.

BETTER TIMES Bobby Hull led the NHL in goals seven times in his 15 seasons with the Blackhawks, a tenure that included five 50-goal seasons.

Instead of finding a way to even come close to Winnipeg's offer, the Wirtzes let Hull leave. Probably not a good decision.

"It's harder to lose somebody in life than in death," Bill Wirtz said later. "Hull had two contracts—one with Winnipeg and one with the WHA—that paid him a total of $2 million. If we (the Blackhawks) sign him for $2 million, what do you pay Stan Mikita and Tony Esposito? And what does another team in the NHL pay its superstars?"

At that moment, the Wirtz-era Hawks changed. Instead of being old-fashioned and careful with money, they were now looked at as simply old and cheap.

Under Bill and Arthur, the Hawks began to stagnate. They made the 1973 Final and again lost to Montreal, but the world was moving beyond their view. More and more teams were putting all their home games on television, a policy Arthur Wirtz detested. When he died in 1983, some hoped Bill would modernize and broadcast everything. Nope.

> "If we (the Blackhawks) sign him for $2 million, what do you pay Stan Mikita and Tony Esposito? And what does another team in the NHL pay its superstars?"
>
> - Bill *WIRTZ*
> OWNER OF THE CHICAGO BLACKHAWKS

Yet despite Bill Wirtz, the 1980s and early 1990s Hawks were a wildly entertaining and relatively successful franchise. They made the 1992 Stanley Cup Final, were a mainstay in the later rounds of the playoffs, and kept fans enthralled with star player after star player. Yet Wirtz wouldn't budge when it came to TV, putting only 1992, 1993, and 1994 home games on a pay-per-view service called HawkVision. So, while fans at home experienced the majesty of Chicago Stadium's roar for Michael Jordan and the Bulls, the only way they could experience the spine-tingling screams after a Blackhawks goal was in person or if they paid enough for PPV, all because of Wirtz's desire to please the "season reservation holders."

Unsurprisingly, the Hawks declined on and off the ice. "Dollar Bill" Wirtz stuck with the same executives who were innovators in the 1980s but fell behind the times in the '90s. Most damningly, as player salaries increased, Wirtz wouldn't budge and pay enough to win a Stanley Cup.

Steve Larmer held out in 1993 and was sent to the New York Rangers. Jeremy Roenick couldn't get the deal he wanted in 1996 and was exiled to Phoenix. Ed Belfour said no to a new contract in 1997 and ended up being traded to San Jose. Most painful, Chris Chelios, the captain and a Chicago-area native, was sent to Detroit in 1999 as the Hawks' window for a Cup closed shut. A 28-year playoff streak ended in 1998, the team made the postseason only once over the next decade, and even the 2001–02 playoff team didn't stay intact as star Tony Amonte left in free agency.

The fervor of Hawks fans cooled. The 20,500-seat United Center, built in 1994 to accommodate the Jordan Bulls and successful Hawks teams, felt emptier and emptier as the product worsened. Fans stayed away in droves. The ones who did come to games were treated more and more shabbily. And on top of everything else, the policy barring home broadcasts was mocked and jeered. The team bought time on a local radio station to air games, but by the 2006–07 season the franchise was an afterthought, drawing an average of only 12,727 per game, 29th in the league. The minor league Wolves openly mocked the Hawks, using this slogan: "We play hockey the old-fashioned way. We actually win." Even beloved announcer Pat Foley wasn't spared; he was dumped in 2006.

In return, fans dumped the team. What was once an unthinkable notion was now understandable.

The Rebirth

Clearly, something needed to change. It did, on September 26, 2007, when Bill Wirtz died of cancer at age 77. Before the Hawks' home opener on October 6, the team paid tribute to Wirtz with a memorial by then-general manager Dale Tallon. Fans booed.

"I told Dale that he should get hazardous-duty pay," Rocky Wirtz, Bill's oldest son, told *Chicago* magazine. "What was hardest was how everyone reacted to it, my sisters and my brother. They were really taken aback. You just take it, and let's get on with it."

Change had arrived, and as booing a dead man showed, Blackhawks fans were ready for something different.

In stepped Rocky Wirtz. Unlike his father, who was fiercely loyal to the old way of doing things, Rocky was eager to mix things up. Immediately, he began working to get some 2007–08 Hawks home games on TV. Team legends Bobby Hull and Stan Mikita were brought back into the fold. Pat Foley was rehired for the 2008–09 season, and Wirtz quickly poached Cubs president and marketing guru John McDonough and tasked him with rebuilding and modernizing the moribund franchise.

"My father was a superb businessman, and he did what he believed was right for the team. But what he really was adamant about was moving the business ahead," Rocky Wirtz told *Chicago*. "So how we get there is going to be different, but he'd be quite happy with the way things are going."

Just as important as any off-ice changes was a new generation of players arriving to change the team's fortunes on the ice. While the business side of the Hawks cratered during the last years of Bill Wirtz's life, the hockey side had begun to assemble some decent prospects. Patrick Sharp, Duncan Keith, and Brent Seabrook were promising, and a core was developing, but the team still needed an anchor.

It got two—taking a center from Winnipeg named Jonathan Toews third overall in the 2006 draft, and a smallish winger from Buffalo named Patrick Kane first overall in 2007.

And when both made their debuts in October 2007, everything changed.

Fans who needed reasons to come back to the Hawks were eager to dust off their red sweaters and return to the United Center. New fans were emerging, and a ticket that once was available for as little as $8 with a student ID was now a cherished piece of paper. A sellout streak that began that March was still going strong into 2018.

Though the 2007–08 season ended just short of a playoff berth, the foundation had been laid. Kane was Rookie of the Year, and 20-year-old Toews was anointed the captain for the 2008–09 campaign, making him the third-youngest captain in NHL history.

Four games into Season 2 of Toews-Kane, the Blackhawks made the controversial choice to fire team legend Denis Savard and hire Joel Quenneville as coach. Now armed with one of the sport's best minds and a roster full of emerging stars, it was only a matter of time before the Hawks won a Cup.

THE DYNASTY'S FIVE MOST
UNDERAPPRECIATED WINS

5. Blackhawks 3, Flames 2 (SO) (February 2, 2013)

The Hawks had picked up at least a point in their first eight games of the lockout-shortened season but looked dead in Calgary. Backup goalie Ray Emery kept the team in the game with 45 saves, giving the Blackhawks a chance to send it to overtime, which they did when Marian Hossa scored with three seconds remaining in the third.

4. Blackhawks 3, Flames 2 (OT) (April 16, 2009)

This was the Hawks' first playoff game in seven seasons, and it was worth the wait. In front of an amped-up United Center crowd, the Hawks tied the score 2–2 on Martin Havlat's goal at 14:27 of the third period. But that wasn't the end of Havlat's heroics. He scored 12 seconds into overtime to give the Hawks a 1–0 series lead and the momentum to carry them to their first series win since 1996.

3. Blackhawks 4, Predators 3 (OT) (April 15, 2015)

Whoever Joel Quenneville throws onto the ice is expected to contribute, and backup goalie Scott Darling did that during the 2015 playoff opener. Playing in place of Corey Crawford, who had given up three first-period goals, Darling was perfect for the final 67:44 of the game and got the victory when Duncan Keith scored at 7:49 of the second overtime.

2. Blackhawks 3, Kings 2 (June 6, 2013)

In Game 4 of the 2013 Western Conference final, Quenneville showed why he might be the game's best coach. Playing without the suspended Keith, Quenneville masterminded an impressive 3–2 win in Los Angeles to give the Hawks a 3–1 series lead. That night, Quenneville made sure the Hawks were a step closer to their second conference title in four seasons.

1. Blackhawks 4, Canucks 2 (May 3, 2010)

The Hawks had dropped Game 1 and fell behind 2–0 five minutes into Game 2. Instead of wilting, the Hawks scored the next four goals to win 4–2 and take back control of the series. What happens if they had lost Game 2? Do they lose the series and the dynasty with it?

It didn't happen in 2009, as the Red Wings beat the Hawks in five games in the Western Conference finals, but that only felt like a prelude after a magical playoff run during which Chicago beat both Calgary and Vancouver in six games, the latter series ending with a Kane hat trick. The season also was memorable from the business side. "Chelsea Dagger" by the Fratellis became the goal song, and on January 1, 2009, the Hawks hosted the Winter Classic at Wrigley Field. That they lost 6–4 to Detroit didn't matter. The Hawks were no longer a sleeping giant. Big events and the Hawks would go together, free agents would flock to Chicago, and the Hawks were now a marquee attraction both on and off the ice.

"To me, that (Winter Classic) changed the DNA of this franchise, absolutely," McDonough said, according to the *Arlington Heights Daily Herald*. "It was a mega event that nobody thought you would get. It reinvigorated this franchise. It gave our fans a feeling that this is really something special that we secured. You look at the environment— no one ever envisioned a game at Wrigley Field. Ever."

Few envisioned what the Hawks would become, or how quickly. Just three years removed from rock bottom, the Hawks won the Stanley Cup on June 9, 2010, in Philadelphia, when Kane beat Flyers goalie Michael Leighton from a bad angle. The celebration in Chicago started soon after and hardly let up for days.

Sure, part of that was just young Chicagoans looking for an excuse to party in the streets and drink all night, but there was more to it. It was the celebration of a franchise that saved itself, and in the process created a whole new generation of fans.

It was a thank-you to Rocky, who deserved to party.

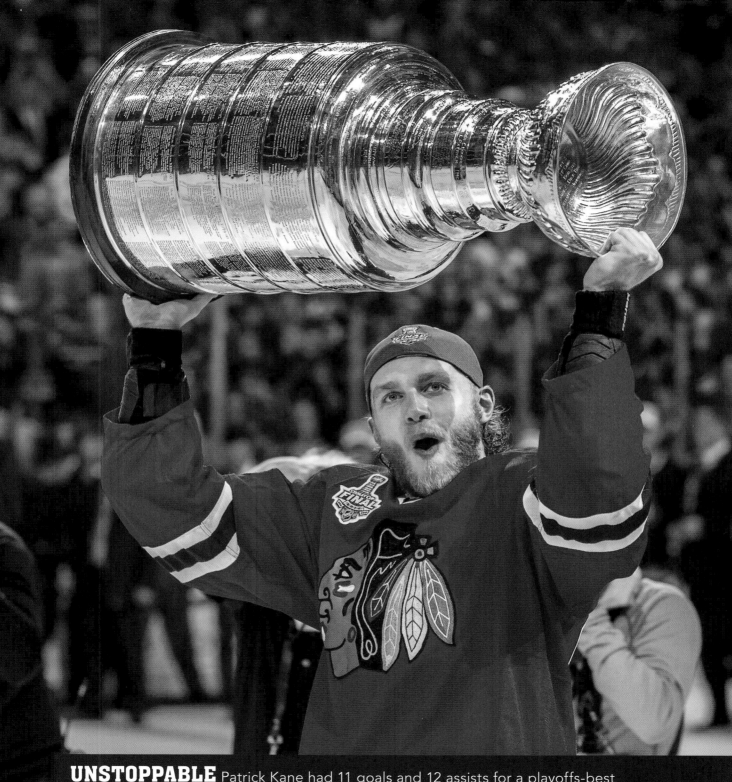

UNSTOPPABLE Patrick Kane had 11 goals and 12 assists for a playoffs-best 23 points, or a point per game, in the 2015 postseason.

The Rivalry: Detroit Red Wings

In 1998, a series of Blackhawks commercials tried to persuade fans to buy tickets. In all honesty, most of the ads were as forgettable as the team, but one stood out.

Wearing an old red Hawks sweater, the actor Jeremy Piven is sitting alone in the upper deck of an empty United Center. He waxes nostalgic about what it meant to see games as a kid with his dad, loving the "camaraderie, the electricity of a big night in the city." Piven, who grew up in Evanston, says everything he knows about life he learned from his father while watching the Hawks. It can all be summed up in "two simple words that ring over and over in my memory: DE-TROIT SUCKS! DE-TROIT SUCKS!"

"Good times," Piven says quietly as the screen rolls to a phone number to buy tickets.

That rivalry, for better or worse, has defined the Blackhawks. For much of their histories, the Hawks and Red Wings were both owned by the Norris family, with the Wings getting preferential treatment. Two of the Hawks' first three Stanley Cup titles (1934, 1961) came by beating the Wings in the Final. And during the Wings' glory years of the mid-1990s and early 2000s, the Hawks and their fans would look longingly at what was happening in Detroit and wish some of that good fortune would spread to Chicago.

Of course, much of it did. Scotty Bowman, coach of three of the Wings' championship teams, joined the Hawks as a senior adviser in 2008. The Hawks' possession-based game soon mimicked the style Detroit used in its heyday, and captain Jonathan Toews is frequently compared to Red Wings legend Steve Yzerman. Even the 2009 Western Conference final, won by Detroit in five games, was viewed as a lesson to the Hawks on what they needed to become to win.

By 2013, the Hawks had become the Wings. They were now the budding dynasty but needed to beat Detroit in the second round of the playoffs to validate their place as the game's model franchise. Yet through four games, the Wings were up 3–1 and poised to ruin the Hawks' charmed season. Then the Hawks won the next two.

Game 7 . . . oh, Game 7. First, Niklas Hjalmarsson's apparent game-winner late in the third period of a 1–1 duel was waved off because of a penalty back up the ice. During the ensuing intermission, Toews rallied his teammates, making sure they weren't despondent over losing what should have been a game-winner. He told his teammates to win 3–1, as if Hjalmarsson's goal had counted. And they did. Brent Seabrook's overtime goal won the game and series and eased the heartache of Hawks fans sick of Detroit spoiling seasons.

"It was a pretty cool moment in our season, in the playoffs, in my life," Seabrook told the *Chicago Sun-Times*. "We've been in a lot of big series and a lot of big games. We've been up; we've been down. All those experiences, you take them into new playoffs, new series, new seasons. It's something you can look back on and lean on and know that, no matter what, we always have a chance."

Unfortunately, in its infinite wisdom, the NHL split up the two Original Six rivals before the 2013–14 season, sending Detroit to the Eastern Conference. Instead of five or six games, the rivals now face each other twice during the regular season and won't face off in the postseason unless they meet in a Stanley Cup Final.

CHICAGO BLACKHAWKS
MOUNT RUSHMORE

Bobby Hull (1957–1972)

No offense to Patrick Kane or Denis Savard, but Hull is the most exciting player in Blackhawks history. Period. Full stop. Nobody else had what he had.

Hull's the one who made the old Chicago Stadium roar. His patented rushes down the ice and blistering slap shot made life hell for opponents and provided the offense for one of the Hawks' golden eras. In 1966, Hull became the first player in NHL history to score more than 50 goals in a season, scoring his 51st on March 12. That accomplishment was just one of many for the Golden Jet in Chicago, as he came to define an era of Blackhawks hockey that was unmatched until the Kane and Jonathan Toews era.

Hull played on the fabled 1961 Hawks team that won the Stanley Cup and starred on the teams that made the Final in 1962, 1965, and 1971. When he left for Winnipeg in 1972, it was the end of an era in Chicago, and something about the franchise was never quite the same.

Patrick Kane (2007–)

Some things Kane does with the puck just defy explanation. Whether it's his ability to dangle, find tiny cracks in the defense, click with linemates, or just bury shots from anywhere, Kane is a unique talent who gives the Hawks the razzle-dazzle they've needed to become a feared offensive team.

Kane was the first overall draft pick in 2007 and overcame doubts about his size to win the Calder Trophy as the NHL's best rookie. That wasn't the last of his awards; he has done just about everything a player can in the NHL, and he has done it with style.

The United Center is known as one of the NHL's loudest venues, but when Kane touches the puck, there's a certain quiet air of anticipation. He's expected to do something spectacular whenever he has possession, and he delivers frequently. Then the UC gets even louder.

Stan Mikita (1959–1980)

What is Mikita's legacy? It could be how he never played for any team other than the Hawks. Maybe it's how he transitioned from a reckless, penalty-prone player into one of the most controlled in the game. He was also as skilled as anybody, winning consecutive Hart trophies. And along with Hull, Mikita was an innovator who changed the game by curving his stick. But perhaps his legacy is how he did all of that with a class and grace that's still remembered to this day.

The story of Mikita is well known, how he came to Canada from the Slovak Republic and blossomed into one of hockey's great ambassadors. What should be appreciated even more is the kind of man he still is. He was named a Blackhawks ambassador and was a perfect fit for the role until the onset of Lewy body dementia robbed him of his memories.

But those memories will live on for everybody else. And everybody should be thankful that Mikita was a hockey player in Chicago.

Jonathan Toews (2007–)

If you're a down franchise looking to rebuild, you can't do any better than having Toews as your centerpiece.

He's the consummate two-way forward who can win a draw, stop a top-scoring line, or produce as well as any forward. More important, he's the real deal when it comes to leadership and handling the media. Toews is the kind of player a franchise needs to transition from loser to winner, and he came along at the perfect time. His accomplishments in the game are too long to list here, but the three Stanley Cup titles and 2010 Conn Smythe Trophy as playoffs MVP represent only a little of what he means to the Hawks and the NHL as a whole.

There's a reason coaches all over the league revere him, and it's not just because he's a great player. He is looked at as an example for players to follow and live up to, as difficult as that might be.

▶ Stan Mikita

47

CHICAGO BLACKHAWKS
BEST OF THE REST

Ed Belfour (1988–1997)

Eddie the Eagle wasn't always the easiest character to deal with, but the goalie stopped enough pucks to make his personality worth it. He won a Calder Trophy and two Vezinas, and he led the Hawks to the 1992 Stanley Cup Final.

Chris Chelios (1990–1999)

His trade to Detroit was a sour ending to a great Chicago career where he played 664 games and went to a Stanley Cup Final, won two Norris Trophies as the league's top defenseman, and became the heart and soul of his hometown team.

Tony Esposito (1969–1983)

"Tony O" won 418 games in goal for the Hawks—along with three Vezina Trophies and one Calder Trophy—and led Chicago to two Stanley Cup Final appearances. For a franchise blessed with great netminders, he might be the best.

Glenn Hall (1957–1967)

"Mr. Goalie" was a mainstay in the Hawks' net during the late 1950s and '60s, leading them to the 1961 Stanley Cup. The Hall of Famer once started 502 consecutive games, a record that won't be broken.

Duncan Keith (2005–)

One of hockey's best two-way defensemen, Keith entered the 2017–18 season having played 913 regular-season games and won three Stanley Cups, two Norris Trophies, and one Conn Smythe. There's no dynasty without Keith.

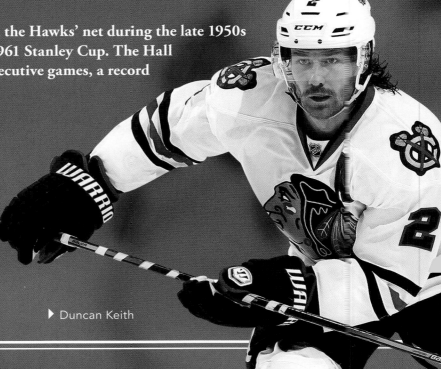

▶ Duncan Keith

Steve Larmer (1980–1993)

Larmer's game wasn't spectacular. He wasn't the fastest skater or the most graceful athlete, but the right wing produced to the tune of 406 goals and 517 assists.

Keith Magnuson (1969–1979)

A defenseman, Magnuson spent all 11 of his NHL seasons with the Hawks and endeared himself to fans, serving 1,442 penalty minutes while playing for two Stanley Cup Final teams (1971, 1973).

Pierre Pilote (1956–1968)

There was no better defenseman in the NHL during the mid-'60s than Pilote. He was a star on the 1961 champions and went on to win three straight Norris Trophies (1963–65) and was named captain for the 1961–62 season.

Joel Quenneville (2008–)

Quenneville's tenure as Blackhawks coach began with the sloppy firing of Denis Savard four games into the 2008–09 season, but few will remember that. What will be remembered are the three Stanley Cups, the constant line-blending, and the glorious moustache.

Jeremy Roenick (1988–1996)

Roenick had all the flair and more than enough toughness to become a star. He left Chicago with 267 goals and a pair of 50-goal seasons when he was sent to Phoenix in 1996, leaving behind more than a few sad Hawks fans.

Denis Savard (1980–1990, 1995–1997)

In the run-and-gun 1980s, Savard thrived. The Hawks never won a Cup with Savard and couldn't get past Edmonton, but his spin-o-rama still lives on in memory. He even helped on his way out, as his trade to Montreal brought Chris Chelios to Chicago.

Doug Wilson (1977–1991)

If Wilson had played on a Stanley Cup champion, his legacy would be even stronger. He won a Norris Trophy in 1982, made eight All-Star Games, and retired as the Hawks' leader in goals and points by a defenseman.

CHAPTER 3
THE
BULLS

Before Michael Jordan and the Bulls, what was Chicago known for internationally? Maybe Al Capone, the 1968 Democratic Convention, and perhaps the stockyards. Now, the Bulls are one of sports' most famous brands, even though Jordan owns a team in another city and the dynasty has been gone for decades. They were ambassadors for a city and gave Chicago an identity as the home of winners.

But to say the Bulls are just Jordan is a shot at their history.

Founded in 1966, the team was expected to fail in a city that was once deemed the graveyard of professional basketball. But unlike their predecessors—the Chicago Stags, American Gears, and Packers/Zephyrs—the Bulls had staying power.

Under Chicago native Johnny "Red" Kerr, the Bulls made the playoffs in their first year and eventually became a contender in the Western Conference.

◀ Michael Jordan hits the game-winning shot against the Utah Jazz during Game 6 of the 1998 NBA Finals.

They never made the NBA Finals in the early days, but the Jerry Sloan–Norm Van Lier–Bob Love–Chet Walker teams had a rugged identity and assured the franchise's survival.

Then came Jordan, Scottie Pippen, and six NBA titles in eight years during the 1990s, a run of dominance that added the Bulls to the list of the NBA's iconic teams, along with the Celtics and Lakers.

Yeah, there have been some down years before and after Jordan, but this franchise will always be an important part of the city. The Bulls play the sport that Chicago does the best. They unite all sides of town and represent the soul of the city.

Much of that is because of what Jordan and his running mates accomplished. But the "Baby Bulls" of Kirk Hinrich, Luol Deng, Eddy Curry, and Tyson Chandler captured the city's hearts in the early 2000s, and then in the early 2010s Derrick Rose, Joakim Noah, Taj Gibson, Tom Thibodeau, and Deng gave Chicago real hope it would win a title for the first time since the dynasty broke up.

They never did, but check out the United Center attendance numbers after Jordan. Not much different than the dynasty days. This is a meaningful franchise and a major reason why Chicago is at the epicenter of American sports.

> "I remember the night of the (1991) championship. I felt we'd win and it was just by how much and then it was like a boulder lifted off everyone. We finally accomplished it and won the title. It was such a relief, joy, the feeling of being on top of the mountain. You are the best and knowing everything you accomplished and went through to get there."
>
> — Cliff **LEVINGSTON**
> BULLS FORWARD (1990—1992)

Jordan and an Iconic Decade

The 1990s Bulls were a phenomenon. They were both rock stars and world-class athletes. Think the Rolling Stones if Mick Jagger had a killer fadeaway and mean competitive streak. There will never be anything like them.

On the court, the 1990s Bulls were without equals.

Everything began and ended with Michael Jordan. He was surrounded by a cast artfully built by general manager Jerry Krause and coached by Phil Jackson. No sidekick was better than Scottie Pippen. Horace Grant and later Dennis Rodman provided the interior toughness and rebounding, and the rest of the support was an eclectic but effective group of role players who did what was needed.

There were the dominant seasons: 61 wins in 1990–91, 67 wins in 1991–92, the historic 72 wins in 1995–96, and the almost-as-good 69-victory team of 1996–97. The playoff runs were dramatic. The 1991 team had to get past the hated Pistons and the fading Lakers to win the first title. The 1992 team rallied from a 15-point deficit to top Portland in Game 6 of the NBA Finals for another title. And in 1993, it was John Paxson's three-pointer that finally vanquished Phoenix and ended a run that included a harrowing victory over the Knicks to win the Eastern Conference.

Then for 18 months or so it stopped, as Jordan retired and became a minor league baseball player. But once he returned in 1995, the phenomenon resumed.

Sure, the Bulls lost to Orlando in the second round of the 1995 playoffs, but that was only a blip before the 1995–96 team dominated in a way no championship team ever had. They won 72 games and were never tested in the playoffs, beating Seattle in six games to win the title and stake a claim as the greatest ever. Jordan's return was validated, and poignantly, on Father's Day.

"I was so determined that day, it was like sometimes you get so angry that you cry. That's how determined I was to win that game. I was so angry and so happy at the same time. There was no way I could control my emotions," said Jordan, who collapsed with emotion in the Bulls' locker room after winning the title. "I was angry because I felt like I had to win another championship before anyone would give credence to my return, but I was happy that I proved my point. I had loved the game for so long and done so much in the game, and yet I was still being criticized. Once I grabbed the ball and the game was over, it hit me as to what had just transpired. I had come all the way back."

By this point, the Bulls were international superstars. Jordan was the pitchman to end all pitchmen and even a movie star after *Space Jam*. Pippen was gaining renown for his all-around game, and Rodman was a tabloid fixture who did everything from staging a fake wedding in New York to kicking a courtside cameraman in the family jewels.

The Bulls were the center of the sports world, and they were damn good.

The legacy only grew in 1997. Although the Bulls fell one win short of another 70-victory season and the playoffs weren't easy, the Finals were historic. Jordan scored 38 points with the flu to retake control of the series in Game 5, and the Bulls punctuated another season with a championship when Steve Kerr hit an open jumper to beat Utah.

THE FIVE GREATEST PLAYS
IN BULLS HISTORY

5. The Shot (May 7, 1989)

Down 100–99 in the final seconds of Game 5 of a 1989 first-round playoff series with Cleveland, Michael Jordan took the inbounds pass from Brad Sellers, hung for a split second longer than poor Craig Ehlo, and . . . good. Jordan pumped his fist over a fallen Ehlo, his teammates raced onto the floor, and a new narrative was written.

4. Pippen and Grant Smother Charles Smith (June 2, 1993)

The Bulls clung to a 95–94 lead with seconds left in Game 5 of the 1993 Eastern Conference finals. The ball found its way to Knicks forward Charles Smith, who was under the basket. Smith went up and was blocked, blocked again, blocked again, and blocked a fourth time by a combination of Scottie Pippen and Horace Grant before Jordan's outlet pass found B.J. Armstrong for a game-ending layup and 97–94 win.

3. Kerr's Open Jumper Wins a Title (June 13, 1997)

If you're going to tell Jordan to pass you the ball with a title on the line, you better not miss. Steve Kerr told Jordan he would be ready if MJ was double-teamed by the Jazz, and he delivered, giving the Bulls their second straight title and fifth in seven seasons. The moment won a championship for the Bulls and also highlighted the growth of Jordan, who at one point in his career never would have given up that shot.

2. Jordan's Greatest Moment (June 14, 1998)

The Bulls were down by three with 41.9 seconds left in Game 6 of the NBA Finals, staring at Game 7 in Utah. Then MJ sliced through the Utah defense for an all-too-easy and all-too-quick layup to make it 86–85. Then he stripped the ball from Karl Malone and dribbled down the court. Bryon Russell met him at the top of the key. Jordan went left and may or may not have shoved Russell before unleashing a perfect 18-footer. Swish. Championship Six.

1. Paxson's Three Gives the Bulls 3 (June 20, 1998)

The Suns had a two-point lead in Game 6 of the 1993 Finals. Game 7 appeared imminent. But the Bulls had the ball. And they began passing the ball, from one Bull's hands to the next, until it got to John Paxson, whose three-pointer rattled in with 3.9 seconds left. That play, drawn up by Phil Jackson, had all five players touch the ball and highlighted all the strengths of the Bulls.

CHAMPS Michael Jordan and Scottie Pippen celebrate with the Larry O'Brien Trophy and MVP trophy after beating the Jazz in the 1997 NBA Finals.

Unfortunately, the end was closer than the beginning, which was borne out by Jackson deeming the season "The Last Dance."

The team was aging, yes, but other cracks were appearing. The relationship between the front office and the players (and Jackson) was dissolving irreparably, Krause was itching to rebuild so the Bulls wouldn't age poorly, and Rodman was becoming more of a headache. The breakup of the Bulls appeared imminent, and as a result fans savored every moment of the last months of the dynasty. At home and on the road, the Bulls played every game in front of full houses. They were mobbed whenever they left the team buses or dared walk in public. Their regular-season games, even against lackluster competition, were must-see TV.

The 1998 Finals, a rematch with Utah, had the vibe of a heavyweight title fight. The great champion on his last legs faced the experienced challenger who never quite reached the top. The first round went to Utah before the Bulls took the next three games. With Game 5 in Chicago, the Bulls had a chance to clinch at home but failed, sending the series back to Salt Lake City.

Game 6 was epic. Back and forth the game went between two great teams before Jordan coolly (and maybe with the help of a push) hit a game-winning jumper to deliver the sixth title. After letting the shot go, he posed for just an extra second to savor his moment, which turned out to be his last in a Chicago uniform.

"Hopefully, I've put enough memories out there," Jordan said.

Michael, you did.

Michael Jordan vs. Everybody

OK, who is the Bulls' greatest rival? The Lakers and Bucks thwarted them in the 1970s, but there hasn't been any hate there for decades. Pistons-Bulls was as intense as any feud in the late 1980s and early 1990s, but that hatred has generally cooled. The Knicks and Bulls constantly battled in the 1990s, though Michael Jordan never lost to New York, and that has faded away. More recently, LeBron James has been a roadblock, and he's done it in two cities. But how about this? The Bulls don't really have one distinct rival, yet Jordan was everybody's.

No team circled Jordan more fiercely than the "Bad Boys" Pistons. They had their "Jordan Rules" to stop him from beating them single-handedly, and that method generally worked, even though the Pistons occasionally denied they existed.

"I don't think we can over concentrate on Michael Jordan," Pistons coach Chuck Daly said in 1990. "If we don't concentrate on him, he's going to get 60 on us."

Once the Bulls got past the Pistons, other challengers were next. In 1993, the Cavaliers acquired Gerald Wilkins to be the "Jordan Stopper." That didn't work, as the Bulls' second-round playoff sweep of Cleveland was punctuated by a Jordan jumper over Wilkins. New York tried to contain Jordan with John Starks, and that worked to a limited extent, as MJ's 54 points in Game 4 of the Eastern Conference finals proved.

Teams would try to go small against Jordan and stymie him with quickness, whether it was Phoenix and Kevin Johnson or Seattle and Gary Payton. Some tried to go big like Atlanta with Steve Smith or, infamously, Utah with Bryon Russell.

Beyond matchups, every team had to compare itself with Jordan, and each of the Finals progressively became a referendum on whoever his challenger was. Clyde Drexler fell short in 1992. Charles Barkley won the 1993 MVP but couldn't stop Jordan from a three-peat. Shaquille O'Neal and the Magic got the best of a rusty Jordan in 1995, but he came back with a vengeance in 1996 and swept Orlando out of the Eastern Conference finals. By 1998, the only challenge Karl Malone and John Stockton hadn't met was Jordan, and they never did, which will forever hurt their legacy. Barkley, Patrick Ewing, and Reggie Miller also know that feeling.

During the 1990s, rivals and challengers came and went, but Jordan was always there. In some ways, he still is. Kobe Bryant spent much of his career emulating Jordan and hearing the comparisons. Though they are different types of players, LeBron will never escape Jordan's shadow and, until he wins six titles, will always pale in comparison for many.

Even the Bulls are a rival of Jordan. Since his retirement, every Bulls star and every Bulls team has suffered in comparison with Jordan. He spoiled the world, the NBA, and definitely Chicago. Derrick Rose and Jimmy Butler were great, but they played in a stadium that has a Jordan statue out front.

Jordan is the standard. He will be a rival to any great player for the rest of time.

Unfulfilled Hope

The Bulls needed Derrick Rose. They just weren't going to get him.

Entering the 2008 draft lottery, the Bulls had a 1.7 percent chance of getting the No. 1 pick they would need to select the Simeon high school product who spent one year at the University of Memphis. After the Baby Bulls faded, the future of the team looked bleak or at least uncertain.

Then . . . holy bleep. The ping-pong balls gave the Bulls what they needed. They also started an exasperating but thrilling adventure.

Instantly, Rose became the Bulls' most exciting player since Jordan. The scrappy and competitive teams of the early and mid-2000s had many admirable traits, but pizzazz wasn't one of them. Immediately, Rose changed the face of the team. He slashed through the lane, jumped with ease, and emerged as the game's most athletic point guard. And to make the story even sweeter, this was a Chicago kid leading the Bulls back to glory.

His first two years led to first-round playoff exits, against the defending-champion Celtics in a memorable seven games in 2009, followed by a five-game exit against LeBron James and Cleveland in 2010. Though the summer of 2010 didn't bring free agent LeBron to Chicago, it brought reinforcements and coach Tom Thibodeau.

The Bulls were ready.

Rose, finally with a credible supporting cast and a top NBA coach, exploded. He averaged 25 points and 7.7 assists per game as the Bulls charged to the league's best record at 62–20. The hometown kid, Rose endeared himself further to the city when he was named NBA MVP and delivered a poignant acceptance speech:

> *Last but not least, I want to thank my mom, Brenda Rose. My heart. The reason that I play the way I play. Just everything. Just knowing that, days I don't feel like going in to practice, when I'm having a hard time. I think about her when she had to wake me up, go to work, and just making sure that I'm all right, and making sure the family's all right. Those are hard days. My days shouldn't be hard because I love doing what I'm doing, and that's playing basketball. You keep me going every day, and I love you, and I appreciate you being in my life.*

Not only was Rose ready to lead the Bulls to a title, but he was genuine.

That title didn't come in 2011, as LeBron's Heat were too big and too athletic for the Bulls, but the title window still appeared wide open. The lockout-shortened 2011–12 season was similar to 2010–11, as the Bulls once again had the league's best record and a favorable first-round matchup with Philadelphia. Late in Game 1 with the Bulls well ahead, Rose drove into the lane and performed a jump stop and . . . oh, no. He was down, holding his left knee.

Later that day, all fears were confirmed. Rose's ACL was torn, and his season was done. So too were the Bulls, who lost in six to Philadelphia. Rose was supposed to come back some time late in the 2012–13 season, but he never did, and for the first time his relationship with the team and city soured. Bulls doctors said he was ready to return, but he didn't, and his desire and motives were questioned.

Rose finally returned in 2013–14 but tore the meniscus in his right knee and, once again, he was finished for the season as the Bulls drifted further from championship contention. They relied on offensive gimmicks and grit and defense to stay competitive, but they were not a true heavyweight without Rose.

Once again, Rose returned in 2014–15, and the Bulls had their last gasp of contention. Despite more controversies, another knee injury, and declining athleticism, Rose took the Bulls to the second round of the playoffs against LeBron's Cavs. He ended Game 3 with a dramatic banked-in three-pointer to give the Bulls a 2–1 series lead, but that was the last playoff game Rose won in Chicago. Cleveland swept the next three, and Thibodeau was fired after the playoffs.

Before the next season, Rose made another curious comment, saying he was already thinking of getting himself right for free agency, which was two years away. Predictably, the comments weren't well received, and it appeared Rose's days in Chicago were numbered. Under new coach Fred Hoiberg, and with Jimmy Butler emerging as the team's best player, the Bulls missed the playoffs. Finally, in the summer of 2016, Rose was traded to New York in a move that would have been unthinkable just a couple of years earlier, ending an era of hope and love and ultimately frustration, and leaving a series of hypotheticals that will never be answered. Rose, if he had won just one title in Chicago, would have been a legend cherished locally in a way no athlete ever has been. Before his injury, he was on a unique path. Unfortunately, that path will be for someone other than Rose.

HAPPIER TIMES Derrick Rose celebrates after a dunk against the New York Knicks in 2012.

CHICAGO BULLS
MOUNT RUSHMORE

Phil Jackson (1989–1998)

It's fair to wonder how much of the Bulls' success in the 1990s was because of Jackson. The team had the greatest player of all time together with the greatest sidekick, plus a supporting cast that was second to none. Yet with Jackson on the bench, the Bulls got everything they could out of the Jordan-Pippen era, and for that he deserves all the acclaim he has gotten.

Sure, Jackson stuck with the triangle offense too long when he was a Knicks executive in later years, but the triangle turned the Bulls from a one-man show into a cohesive unit. Once Jordan was convinced it would work, the triangle helped turn the Bulls' offense into an unstoppable force.

Perhaps Jackson's greatest accomplishment was massaging the egos of Jordan, Pippen, Horace Grant, Dennis Rodman, and the rest of the rock star Bulls. He let them be themselves but kept them together just enough to win six titles in eight seasons and become the NBA's greatest modern dynasty.

Michael Jordan (1984–1993, 1995–1998)

The greatest basketball player of all time. The most influential athlete of all time. The most revolutionary sports figure of all time.

And yet, that's only a sliver of Jordan's legacy.

He was great when it didn't matter and nobody was watching, and even better when the game was on the line in front of millions of people. He gave the city of Chicago a new definition, not to mention what he did for the Bulls, the NBA, and his corporate partners. Jordan was a heaven-sent dream that turned every Bulls fantasy into reality. Nobody will match Jordan now or in 100 years. He scored 63 points in a playoff game in Boston, won an NBA Finals game while battling the flu, and gave every fan who watched something to remember him by.

"Michael Jordan is the greatest player of all time," Dwyane Wade said in a 2016 interview with ESPN. "That's who everyone shoots for."

Scottie Pippen (1987–1998, 2003–2004)

Pippen doesn't have a perfect Bulls legacy. His migraine in Game 7 of the 1990 Eastern Conference finals was a bad look, and he never completely lived down staying on the bench for the final 1.8 seconds of a crucial 1994 playoff game because he wasn't getting the last shot, but Pippen's career in Chicago was still remarkable.

A fun fact about Pippen's career is that Jordan never won a playoff series without him. And anybody who watched Pippen play would know why. He was a terrific defensive player who used his rangy body to harass opponents. His offensive game evolved, and he turned into one of the first "point forwards" who could bring the ball up and run an offense despite his 6'8" frame.

Pippen's game was unique, and his legacy grows better with age. Though it might not be as remembered as his six titles, Pippen's best season might have been 1993–94, when he dragged the Bulls to 55 wins without Jordan and came within a blown call in the second round of the playoffs of beating the Knicks and maybe winning a title while MJ played baseball.

Jerry Sloan (1966–1976, player, 1979–1982, coach)

If you're a fan who came of age in the 1990s, you only know Sloan as the white-haired coach of the Utah Jazz who could never quite figure out how to beat the Bulls in two NBA Finals. That's nowhere close to his biggest contribution to the franchise.

Known as the "Original Bull" after he was acquired in the 1966 expansion draft from the Baltimore Bullets, Sloan defined the first decade of Bulls basketball with his tenacity and tough defense. He was the on-court leader of the team and one of the best players on a group that contended in the Western Conference but never won a championship.

"Jerry Sloan was probably one of the most tenacious competitors that I've ever seen," Pistons legend Bob Lanier said. "He'd get in your jockstrap and ride you all the way down the court."

▶ Scottie Pippen

CHICAGO BULLS
BEST OF THE REST

Jimmy Butler (2011–2017)

No Bulls player did more to make himself great than Butler. Drafted No. 30 overall, Butler turned into an All-Star and Olympic gold medalist before being dealt in 2017 to start the franchise's latest post-Jordan rebuild. He will be appreciated more and more as time goes by, because he was truly one of the few self-made NBA superstars.

Bill Cartwright (1988–1994)

Michael Jordan wasn't happy when buddy Charles Oakley was traded to New York for Cartwright, but the deal brought the final piece to the championship puzzle. Cartwright provided the strong defensive center the Bulls needed, and he was the heart of a defense that won three championships.

Artis Gilmore (1976–1982, 1987)

The Bulls haven't been a franchise that has been blessed with great centers, but Gilmore is the best of the bunch. He averaged more than 22 points per game twice and was the star of the 1976–77 "Miracle on Madison Street" team.

Horace Grant (1987–1994)

One of Jerry Krause's great draft picks, Grant meshed quickly with Scottie Pippen to form one of the NBA's most athletic frontcourts. A member of the first three championship teams, Grant's all-around game was sorely underappreciated in its time.

Steve Kerr (1993–1998)

Kerr was brought in to space the floor and provide decent minutes as a backup point guard. He did much more than that, winning three championships and hitting the title-winning shot in 1997. Chicago served as a springboard for Kerr, who won two more titles with the Spurs, became an insightful announcer, and later emerged as a wildly successful coach with the Warriors. He also won plaudits for his sense of humor, which he showed at the team's 1997 championship rally as he recounted a play.

"We called timeout with 25 seconds to go, went into the huddle, Phil told Michael, 'Michael, I want you to take the last shot.' And Michael said, 'Phil, I don't feel real comfortable in these situations, so maybe we ought to go in another direction.'"

Bob Love (1968–1976)

A dangerous scorer on the oh-so-close teams of the 1970s, Love emerged as a great all-around player during his time with the Bulls. His profile would be significantly higher if his Bulls teams had ever broken through to win a title or at least make an NBA Finals.

Dennis Rodman (1995–1998)

"The Worm" was flamboyant, hard to control, and, well, a little bit off, but the dude could play. He was the final piece to the puzzle for the second three-peat and will go down as one of the greatest rebounders in NBA history. He was a headache and prone to bad behavior, but when it mattered, Rodman usually delivered.

Derrick Rose (2008–2016)

The city saw itself in Rose. A product of the South Side, Rose was an MVP and the Bulls' best player since Jordan until his knees and spirit gave out. One of the greatest "what-ifs" in Chicago sports history. Even in the blizzard of injury and controversy, it will be hard to lose sight of his explosive athleticism.

▶ Steve Kerr

CHAPTER 4
THE CUBS

What are the Chicago Cubs as a franchise? For some, they're still the cutesy team with the ivy-covered ballpark that put their fans through hell. To more and more people, they're the burgeoning power of baseball that boasts a trove of stars and maybe the best front office and ownership in the sport.

Regardless, they are a team that has been intertwined with its city.

The Cubs have represented Chicago in one form or another since 1876 and have been an embodiment of the Second City. Their fans have never given up, and in return they have watched a team play in the most beautiful ballpark in America and listened to great voices such as Harry Caray, Jack Brickhouse, and current announcers Pat Hughes and Len Kasper.

◀ Nobody represented the North Side quite like "Mr. Cub" Ernie Banks.

Sure, the Cubs have had their downers. Those 108 years without a championship weren't always filled with beautiful baseball. But there have been plenty of exhilarating experiences for Cubs fans.

> "A pessimist sees the glass as half empty; A Cub fan wonders when it's gonna spill."
>
> - Mike *ROYKO*
> LONGTIME CHICAGO NEWSPAPER COLUMNIST

In 1906, the team had a record of 116–36, which is still the best in MLB history based on winning percentage. And though that team lost in the World Series, falling to the White Sox, the Cubs won back-to-back championships in 1907 and 1908. Gabby Hartnett's "Homer in the Gloamin'" propelled the North Siders to another pennant in 1938. Lights shined down on Wrigley for the first time in 1988. And who can forget the epic 1998 home run race that captivated the baseball world?

All the while, iconic players dotted just about every generation of Cubs. Those early 1900s teams featured legends the likes of Joe Tinker, Johnny Evers, and Frank Chance. "Mr. Cub" Ernie Banks arrived in 1953, and soon after so did Ferguson Jenkins, Ron Santo, and Billy Williams. Ryne Sandberg ruled the 1980s before giving way to "Slammin'" Sammy Sosa in the 1990s. Now a new generation of stars, led by Kris Bryant and Anthony Rizzo, has only continued that tradition.

Through everything, the Cubs and their fans have been in love with each other for almost 150 years. Even through the worst of the worst, the relationship between Chicago and the Cubs has been a phenomenon.

A Curse, a Drought, and Perseverance

Before 2016, the Cubs and heartbreak went together like Chicago and deep-dish pizza. When you thought of one, the other popped into your head. But Cubs fans have always stood by their team. Even when games or seasons were hopeless, Cubs fans would be there to cheer. For better or worse, the Cubs could always depend on their fans.

But damn, there was a lot of worse. There were the seven straight World Series losses from 1910 to 1945, Babe Ruth supposedly calling his shot in 1932, and the years of frustration as failures in October built up, but the heartbreak really started in 1945 when the Cubs lost the World Series to Detroit in seven games. The Curse of the Billy Goat began when a local bar owner tried to take his goat into Wrigley and was promptly booted out of the park. Whether or not you believe in that sort of thing, something changed with the Cubs.

Once a National League power, they became also-rans. Players would get good when they left and get bad when they came. To pour more salt on the festering wound, whenever the team looked as if it would have a chance to win, fans gave the players all the love they could. But that too often backfired.

In 1969, on August 16, the Cubs led the NL East by nine games.

"There was no way we weren't going to win," Ron Santo said.

Then the bottom fell out. By the time the Cubs went to New York for a two-game series with the Mets on September 8–9, they were just 2 ½ games up and in the middle of what ended up as an eight-game skid. They left just a half-game in front, and the lead was gone for good by September 10 as the Miracle Mets went on to win the division, the pennant, and the World Series.

But even falling short, that Cubs team is beloved now and was adored then. The Bleacher Bums were always whipped into a frenzy, and the team's best players are legends of the franchise to this day.

The 1984 team knows the feeling.

It went 96–65 and reached the postseason for the first time in 39 years. The campy "Go Cubs Go"—though composer and performer Steve Goodman hated it—became an anthem for fans. And for the first time since the early 1970s, the Cubs were cool. Harry Caray was hawking Budweiser, fans across the country saw every game on WGN, and it was only a matter of time before the Cubs and the Detroit Tigers would meet in the 1984 World Series.

"It's been fun to watch the businessmen coming to the park after work for three o'clock Friday games," longtime White Sox owner Bill Veeck said. "Three-piece suits and an attaché case. The coat and vest go in the case and out comes the Cubs cap."

Yet, well, that date with the Tigers didn't happen. The Cubs lost three straight in San Diego, and their best chance to win a pennant in 40 years evaporated. But even today, Ryne Sandberg is effectively a club ambassador, Gary Matthews and Rick Sutcliffe are still beloved, and the 1984 team was a signal that it was possible for the Cubs to contend.

By 2003, the Cubs were one of baseball's most beloved teams despite having won nothing in six decades. Tickets at Wrigley Field were hard to come by, and the franchise was one of baseball's jewels. All it needed to become the face of the sport was a title.

This year, as Santo loved to say, was the year. Dusty Baker, Mark Prior, Kerry Wood, Sammy Sosa, and Moises Alou had the Cubs on the verge of a pennant. Fans who couldn't get into the games stood outside the bleachers just to be in the area when it happened. And they were there

▲ Gary Matthews and the 1984 Cubs were surely on their way to the World Series until they weren't.

when it didn't happen. The team fell apart late in Game 6 of the 2003 NLCS and faded away the next night.

There are famous photos of tearful Cubs fans sitting in Wrigley Field after the Game 7 loss to Florida. Some cried openly, others stared forward in shock, but all felt the pain only possible if you lived and breathed with the franchise.

But through all of that, Cubs fans were there. They never stopped believing in the next move, the next manager, or the next big free-agent signing. Part of being a Cubs fan was being part of a community that believed that eventually something good was coming and that the faith was going to be repaid eventually.

Finally

It's hard to imagine a team meaning more to its fans than the 2016 Cubs. This was the group of players Cubs fans had been waiting for. It had the matinee idol with the talent in slugger Kris Bryant, the emotional heart that was first baseman Anthony Rizzo, the veteran leadership and steadiness of ace Jon Lester, and the pragmatic but revolutionary leadership of manager Joe Maddon and team president Theo Epstein.

It also won the World Series in the most gut-wrenching way possible.

There had been a theory that the Cubs would finally win it all when they weren't expected to. That the only way they could do it was when there was no pressure or expectations, that it would be a pleasant surprise sprung by a group of underdogs. The 2016 Cubs were not this. After a 97-win season and a run to the 2015 NLCS, the Cubs were everybody's pick to win the 2016 World Series. They knew it and enjoyed it.

"We're embracing the target," Maddon said. "That's where we're going with this whole thing. Sometimes expectations and pressure are actually positive words. That means there's the opportunity to do something very good."

Oh, the Cubs did something very good. They started 25–6 and, with the exception of a rough run before the All-Star break, they cruised to their first division title since 2008. Bryant went from Rookie of the Year to MVP, Lester and Kyle Hendricks were Cy Young candidates, and the Cubs entered the playoffs as favorites to finally win the World Series.

Unlike other years, they responded.

They led the Giants two games to one in the NL Division Series, but entered the ninth inning of Game 4 down 5–2. A loss would have sent the series back to Chicago for a decisive Game 5 against ace Johnny Cueto. Cubs fans were thinking the worst. The Cubs themselves? They rallied against the Giants' bullpen and won the series, making people believe they had more than just talent but the heart and resiliency to finally do it.

▲ Anthony Rizzo reacts after hitting a double against the Dodgers in Game 6 of the NLCS.

Up next were the Dodgers. The Cubs won Game 1 at a raucous Wrigley Field thanks to an eighth inning grand slam by Miguel Montero, but then the bats fell silent. Two games, no runs, lots of panic by the fans. The Cubs responded to win the next three games, toppling Clayton Kershaw in Game 6 at Wrigley to finally win the pennant.

"This is as special as it gets in sports," Rizzo said. "I know my parents are crying. I know my girlfriend is crying. Everyone's crying."

Cubs fans cried, too. They finally saw their team win the pennant—and, even better, at Wrigley. Wrigley Field was becoming something of a holy place. Fans made pilgrimages just to be in the neighborhood, and they began leaving messages on the outer wall with chalk.

This team, this special group, was four wins away from ending all talk of 1908 forever, and all the Cubs needed to do was topple a beat-up underdog Cleveland Indians. It would be easy, right?

No.

Through four games, Cleveland led 3–1. The Cubs' offense went silent at the worst time, and the Indians looked like the better team. After 103 wins and the pennant, the 2016 Cubs appeared doomed to end their run as an incomplete book, lacking the final killer chapter.

Led by Lester and Bryant and closer Aroldis Chapman, the Cubs won Game 5 to send the series back to Cleveland. After Addison Russell's grand slam, Game 6 was a cakewalk that set up a game and date—November 2—that no Cubs fan will ever forget.

Game 7. It had to be Game 7. No way the Cubs and their fans would get what they wanted without the greatest amount of pain and suffering. Early on, the Cubs controlled the game. Dexter Fowler led off with a homer, the beloved David Ross also went deep, and Chicago led 6–3 in the eighth inning with Chapman on the mound.

Then . . . oh, my God. With Chapman's stuff down a notch, he allowed Rajai Davis's game-tying, two-run homer in the bottom of the eighth. After 108 years of pain, this would be the worst heartbreak yet. So close and yet nothing, and Cubs fans felt it. Twitter blew up, fathers called their sons to vent about what happened, and others just couldn't bear to watch what was happening.

Somehow, Chapman got through the ninth inning. Before the 10th started, the skies opened up for a 17-minute rain delay. During the break, right fielder Jason Heyward led an

FINALLY After extra innings in Game 7, Kris Bryant and the Cubs were finally, after 108 years, World Series champions.

emotional team meeting that will go down in history. And when the game restarted, the Cubs came out swinging. Ben Zobrist and Montero drove in runs, and the Cubs led 8–6. Three outs left. But, of course, things got sticky.

After reliever Carl Edwards Jr. allowed a run, he was replaced by Mike Montgomery. With a runner on and two outs, Montgomery got Michael Martinez to ground to third. Bryant charged, and his foot appeared to slip as he threw. For a split second, the same feeling of dread went through every Cubs fan's mind: The ball would sky over Rizzo, the tying run would score, and the Indians would win.

No. The ball nestled easily in Rizzo's glove. The Cubs were champions.

The players celebrated, and so did the fans. They went to graves of relatives and friends who didn't live to see the triumph, they called their loved ones, and some just reflected on what happened.

It happened.

THE FOUR MOST FUN TEAMS
IN CUBS HISTORY

The 2016 or 1907 and 1908 teams are too easy, but these teams also live on for Cubs fans.

4. The Dominance of 2008

The 2008 Cubs were loaded with power bats and power arms and a flair for the dramatic. The fun started in April and included comeback wins and a joyride through the NL for a league-best 97 wins. The fun ended for manager Lou Piniella and the Cubs in a three-game sweep by the Dodgers in the NLDS.

3. The Boys of Zimmer (1989)

Don Zimmer was back as manager, and the team had dealt a prospect named Rafael Palmeiro to Texas in a big trade for Mitch Williams. But very quickly, the team came together. Starter Mike Bielecki had a career season, and Greg Maddux emerged as a true ace. Center fielder Jerome Walton was the rookie of the year, and Ryne Sandberg, Mark Grace, Andre Dawson, Dwight Smith, and late acquisition Luis Salazar gave the "Boys of Zimmer" enough offense to win the East. However, the experienced Giants ended the Cubs' season in a five-game rout in the NLCS.

2. The Duel of 1998

Kerry Wood won rookie of the year thanks to 13 victories and his 20-strikeout game against Houston. Sammy Sosa, who had never become a true superstar, exploded with a 20-homer June to begin one of baseball's greatest home run races. In the end, Mark McGwire won the home run title 70–66, but the Cubs survived Brant Brown's drop of a fly ball against Milwaukee to reach a wild-card playoff against the Giants, where they won 5–3. Atlanta ended the Cubs' season with a three-game sweep in the NLDS.

1. 2015 Was the Beginning

After winning 73 games in 2014, the 2015 Cubs won 97 and claimed the second wild card as the core of Theo Epstein's rebuild was coming together. In the NL wild-card game at Pittsburgh, Jake Arrieta threw a complete-game shutout, and Kyle Schwarber homered for the win, setting up the cataclysmic NLDS with St. Louis. In the teams' first playoff matchup, the Cubs won in four games, with Schwarber's Game 4 homer over the video board in right field putting an exclamation point on the triumph. Though the Mets swept Chicago out of the NLCS, nobody was too disturbed.

The Rivalry: St. Louis Cardinals

When Theo Epstein and Jed Hoyer took over the Cubs in 2011, they talked about turning the franchise into a team that could win every year because of how it developed players through its minor league system. Though some might not have liked it, the implication was clear: They wanted to mimic the Cardinals.

"Every great organization has a way of doing things, going back to the Dodger Way and their great stability," Hoyer said in 2016. "They had the Dodger Way of teaching, and then the Oriole Way. The Cardinal Way has gotten a lot of attention, and it should. They've done a great job teaching fundamentals and in player development.

"Ultimately that's the way we see it, teaching our players how to play fundamentally and how we want them to play."

The Cubs-Cardinals rivalry was born in 1892, and, believe it or not, the Cubs held a 1,221–1,161 lead all time entering the 2018 season. But when it comes to World Series titles and pennants, the Cardinals have the edge, and their fans will always remind you of that fact. Yet, as much as Cubs fans resent it, there's a good reason the Cardinals have more trophies.

They've been a consistently well-run franchise for more than a century.

Thanks to Branch Rickey pioneering the modern farm system for the Cardinals in the 1920s, St. Louis has a well-established tradition of player development and scouting.

One Cardinals star comes in and replaces the next, and that has been something the Cubs have struggled with historically. There is no better example of this than the 1964 trade that sent Lou Brock to the Cardinals

for a sore-armed veteran pitcher named Ernie Broglio. At the time of the deal, Brock was foundering, but he became a different player as soon as he put on a red cap, while Broglio's arm gave out and led to the trade becoming one of the worst in baseball history.

By the time of that trade, the Cubs-Cardinals divide was wide, and the divide only got wider. The Cubs had strong teams in the late 1960s and early 1970s but never got over the hump, while Brock went to three World Series with St. Louis and won two.

Two years after the Cardinals beat Milwaukee to win the 1982 title, the Cubs were finally a contender, and the teams met on June 23, 1984, on national television. Built by GM Dallas Green, the 1984 Cubs were a hodgepodge of veterans meant to play decent baseball before Green's rebuild bore fruit. On that day, Ryne Sandberg hit a pair of game-tying homers in a game the Cubs won to stake their claim as the best team in the NL East.

It was also against the Cardinals, which made it even sweeter.

Of course, the Cubs didn't end their title drought in 1984, and then they had to watch as the Cardinals won pennants in 1985 and 1987. The home run duel between Sosa and the Cardinals' Mark McGwire in 1998 was fun and historic but did little to flip the balance of the rivalry. The fans hated each other, loved the rivalry, and enjoyed invading the other's ballpark, but it was still the Cubs chasing the Cardinals.

Then, in 2003, the Cubs were back in contention and met the Cardinals for a key five-game series in September at Wrigley Field. The Cubs won four of the five on their way to a division title. Perhaps, finally, they had turned the tables on the Cardinals.

Well, no.

We all know how the 2003 season ended for the Cubs, and St. Louis—under Tony LaRussa and led by Albert Pujols, Scott Rolen, and a cast of terrific role players—won the 2004 pennant, the 2006 and 2011 World Series, and another NL flag in 2013, while the Cubs had been ousted twice in the NLDS and were further than ever from their rival down in Missouri.

By 2011, something needed to change with the Cubs. Epstein and Hoyer knew it, so they went about building a farm system like the Cardinals'. It would develop stars and tradable assets and keep the Cubs' shelves stocked with talent, and combined with their money, would allow them to overtake St. Louis now and for the foreseeable future.

Unlike other Cubs plans, this one worked. The young and dynamic Cubs, three years removed from a 101-loss season, met the Cardinals in a best-of-five NLDS. After dropping Game 1, the Cubs took over. Led by players acquired via great trades and solid free-agent signings, and ones they themselves had drafted and developed, the Cubs were a complete team. The coup de grâce came in Game 4 when Kyle Schwarber blasted a homer to propel the Cubs past the Cardinals into the NL Championship Series.

"This is all just baseball fantasy, right?" owner Tom Ricketts said after the win.

It was real. The Cubs had beaten the Cardinals in a playoff series. And, finally, they were the top dog in the rivalry. How did they do it? By emulating the Cardinals.

CHICAGO CUBS
MOUNT RUSHMORE

Ernie Banks (1953–1971)

Banks broke into the big leagues in 1953 and was the Cubs' first black player. He quickly emerged as one of the sport's best and most dynamic players at shortstop. Despite the Cubs finishing well out of contention both seasons, Banks was the NL MVP in 1958 and 1959, which was even more impressive because by the voting standards of the day winners predominantly came from the best teams.

By the mid-1960s, Banks was a full-time first baseman and veteran on an emerging team. By the time he hit his 500th homer on May 12, 1970, he was well past his prime but on his way to becoming a true living legend. Though a World Series eluded him, Banks lives on in baseball history and received one of the country's greatest honors in 2013 when he received a Presidential Medal of Freedom.

Frank Chance (1898–1912, manager 1905–1914, 1923),
Johnny Evers (1902–1913, manager 1921), Joe Tinker (1902–1912, 1916)

They were immortalized in "Baseball's Sad Lexicon," the 1910 poem by New York Giants fan Franklin Pierce Adams, who was sick of seeing these three turn double play after double play against his favorite team.

But poetry aside, these three were the hearts of the Cubs' dynasty of the early 1900s, helping the team win a record-116 games in 1906, reach four World Series in five years from 1906 to 1910, and take home back-to-back titles in 1907 and 1908.

Chance, the first baseman, was also the manager of that powerhouse from 1905 to 1912 and led the NL in stolen bases twice and runs scored once. Though Joe Maddon could overtake him eventually, Chance is undisputedly the most successful manager in Cubs history. Evers, the second baseman, was a bit of a hothead but renowned for his baseball smarts and intelligence, which showed when he alerted umpires to Fred Merkle's infamous base-running mistake in 1908. Tinker, the shortstop, was one of the NL's steadiest players during his era, despite a feud with Evers.

Apart, these three are important figures in Cubs history.

Together, as they always will be in history, they are titans.

Anthony Rizzo (2012–)

The acquisition of Rizzo from San Diego was the first big move made by Theo Epstein, and the beginning of what could be the greatest era of Cubs baseball. Though he has been somewhat overshadowed on the diamond by Kris Bryant, Rizzo is the unquestioned leader of the Cubs. He sets the tone with his fun-loving personality when things need to be light, but he's also a dedicated professional who takes his craft seriously.

Rizzo's story of overcoming cancer is an inspirational one, and he has put his time and money where his mouth is when it comes to that terrible disease. Rizzo has donated millions of dollars to local causes and spent hours hanging out and having fun with juvenile cancer patients.

Rizzo is the real deal. He has made Chicago his own, and Chicago has responded to the big first baseman. He's one of a kind and will leave a legacy to be proud of, both on and off the field.

Ryne Sandberg (1982–1994, 1996–1997)

Sandberg came to the Cubs as a raw infielder tacked on to a deal with Philadelphia. He became one of the steadiest second basemen ever and the 1984 NL MVP, leading the Cubs to within a game of the World Series.

It was during that magical '84 season when Sandberg began cementing his Cubs legacy. On June 23 against the Cardinals and in front of a national NBC audience with Bob Costas on the call, Sandberg hit game-tying homers in the ninth and 10th innings off future Hall of Famer Bruce Sutter to lead the Cubs to a wild 12–11 victory in what will always be known as the "Sandberg Game."

Sandberg retired in 1994, came back in 1996, and left for good after the next season. He worked his way through the Cubs' minor-league system as a manager but never got the call to Wrigley. He eventually managed the Phillies but resigned and returned to Chicago, where he's grown into a role as a franchise ambassador.

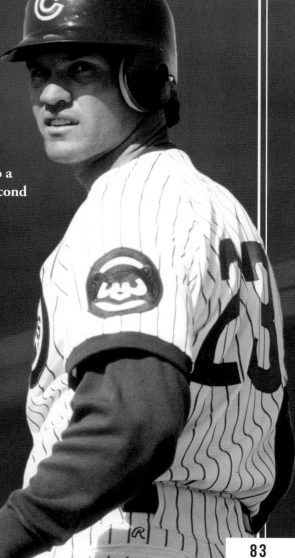

▶ Ryne Sandberg

83

CHICAGO CUBS
BEST OF THE REST

Cap Anson (1876–1897)

As a player, Anson was one of the finest in team history, retiring with around 3,000 hits, mostly as a first baseman. However, his legacy is severely diminished by his role in building baseball's color barrier that wasn't broken until 1947.

Mordecai "Three Finger" Brown (1904–1912, 1916)

Brown was the ace of the Cubs' first two World Series champions and did it with a mangled right index finger. He won 20 games or more six times for the Cubs, and led the NL in ERA in 1906. "I always felt if I had had a normal hand, I would have been a greater pitcher," he said.

Kris Bryant (2015–)

Talk about a fast start. Bryant went from the NL Rookie of the Year in 2015 to the NL MVP in 2016. Drafted by the Cubs second overall in 2013, the third baseman proved to be everything the Cubs expected him to be and more. On the field and also off the field, few players were better suited to lead a franchise than Bryant.

Phil Cavarretta (1934–1953)

A four-time batting All-Star and 1945 NL MVP, Cavarretta was Mr. Cub before Ernie Banks. He played in three World Series for the Cubs, and his 20 seasons with the franchise are the second-most for any player, and his last three were as a player-manager.

Grover Cleveland Alexander (1918–1926)

Alexander had his greatest glories with the Phillies and won a World Series with the Cardinals, but he had some terrific years in between with the Cubs. He won the pitching Triple Crown in 1920 with 27 wins, a 1.91 ERA, and 173 strikeouts, and had other strong seasons before going to St. Louis in 1926.

Gabby Hartnett (1922–1940)

Hall of Fame catchers are hard to come by, and Hartnett was one of the best. The 1935 NL MVP, Hartnett will forever be known for his 1938 "Homer in the Gloamin'." With night descending on Wrigley Field and an 0-and-2 count in the bottom of the ninth, Hartnett blasted the ball into the darkness, propelling the Cubs to the NL pennant three days later.

Ferguson Jenkins (1966–1973, 1982–1983)

Jenkins was the definition of an ace. He won the 1971 NL Cy Young Award and picked up at least 20 victories in six consecutive seasons. In 10 seasons with the Cubs, Jenkins had 154 complete games, including 30 during a 1971 season that saw him start 39 times.

Joe Maddon (2015–)

Theo Epstein made a lot of good decisions upon his arrival in 2011. Hiring Maddon was a no-brainer, and the results speak for themselves. With his new-age sensibilities and old-school love of the game, Maddon created a culture that brought home the 2016 World Series title.

Ron Santo (1960–1973)

Santo was beloved by one generation of fans for his standout play at third base, which earned him nine All-Star nods, and another for being the loud and passionate color man on Cubs radio broadcasts who will forever be known for his guttural "NOOO!!!" after Brant Brown's drop in 1998. Unfortunately, Santo wasn't alive for his bittersweet and overdue Hall of Fame induction in 2012.

Sammy Sosa (1992–2004)

If this were based solely on numbers, Sosa would be the greatest Cubs player of all time. Unfortunately, there's much more to his legacy than home runs, hops, and kisses. Still, he was one of baseball's most exciting and famous players at a time the sport needed pizzazz. His clutch homer to tie Game 1 of the 2003 NLCS would have a bigger spot in team history if the Cubs hadn't lost the game and the series.

Billy Williams (1959–1974)

The sweet-swinging Williams was the 1961 NL Rookie of the Year, a six-time All-Star, and the 1972 NL batting champ with the Cubs. The sight of Williams soaking in the Cubs' 2016 pennant on the field at Wrigley will not be forgotten.

▶ Ferguson Jenkins

CHAPTER 5
THE WHITE SOX

There's an urge for people to call the White Sox Chicago's South Side team. The White Sox are much more than that. They're a charter American League franchise with a colorful history, iconic characters, and three World Series championships. They don't need to be marked by what part of town they play in.

They're the Chicago White Sox, and that speaks for itself.

The White Sox pulled one of the great World Series upsets, beating the 116-win Cubs with a bunch of hitless wonders to win the 1906 title. They're the 1917 champions and the 1919 Black Sox, who have become more than a team. The Black Sox live on in popular culture, whether it's in *Field of Dreams* or *Eight Men Out* or even the reference to Meyer Wolfsheim fixing the 1919 World Series in *The Great Gatsby*. But the White Sox are still much more than that.

◀ Paul Konerko pumps his fist after hitting a grand slam in Game 2 of the 2005 World Series against the Houston Astros.

The first All-Star Game was held in 1933 at Comiskey Park, and the Beatles performed there in their heyday. The black hat the Sox wear is an iconic fashion statement. But the Sox still mean even more than that. They can claim the Old Roman Charles Comiskey, Shoeless Joe, Luke Appling, Ted Lyons, Nellie Fox and his big wad of chaw, Little Luis Aparicio, and the Go-Go Sox who won the 1959 pennant with a colorful owner named Bill Veeck.

Dick Allen, Harry Caray, and Veeck again made the 1970s great with their colorful uniforms and even more colorful personalities, not to mention the South Side Hitmen and Disco Demolition Night.

Carlton Fisk, Harold Baines, and Ozzie Guillen defined the next era, one that bled from Old Comiskey to the new Comiskey Park. The 1993 White Sox won their division, and the 1994 team could have won more as Frank Thomas became the game's most feared right-handed hitter during that strike-shortened season. Six years later, "The Kids Can Play" team of 2000 added another division title, and then the 2005 grinders ended 88 years of heartbreak with an 11–1 postseason.

Even in lesser seasons, there's reason to watch. In 2009, Mark Buehrle threw a perfect game, and three years later Phil Humber did so too, giving the Sox three—along with Charlie Robertson's from 1922. The Yankees can match that feat, but no team has more perfect games.

So needless to say, the Sox will always give Chicago reasons for pride. That's why they're an indispensable part of the city.

The Black Sox

It's the most infamous moment in World Series history. Favored to easily win the 1919 championship, the White Sox lost in eight games to a Cincinnati Reds team that should have been overmatched. Rumors swirled and investigations were opened, and though nobody was convicted, commissioner Kenesaw Mountain Landis banned eight players, consigning them to the pits of baseball.

"Shoeless" Joe Jackson. Eddie Cicotte. Lefty Williams. Buck Weaver. Chick Gandil. Swede Risberg. Happy Felsch. Fred McMullin. The eight names will be bonded together in history for what happened during that Series with Cincinnati.

Though the Sox won only 88 games (eight fewer than Cincinnati), they were the bettors' choice to win the title for the second time in three seasons. Jackson was in his prime, having hit .351. Weaver, Risberg, Gandil, and Eddie Collins gave the Sox the best infield in baseball, and Felsch was strong in center field. Cicotte won 29 games, Williams added 23, and Sox fans thought they had two pitchers who could stymie the Reds.

Of course, that's not what happened. Cicotte signaled to gamblers the fix was in by hitting the first Reds batter in the lopsided Game 1 loss. Williams was just good enough to lose Game 2, and after five games the Sox were down 4–1 as most of the implicated players made suspiciously poor plays.

Still alive thanks to the expanded best-of-nine format, the Sox won the next two games and returned to Comiskey for Game 8 finally holding some momentum. That ended when the Reds battered Williams for four runs in the first inning on their way to a 10–5 win to clinch the Series.

Throughout the 1920 season, the whispers grew louder and louder about what had happened in the fall of 1919. In late September and with the Sox back in the pennant race, the accused were finally suspended. Angry at low pay from owner Charles Comiskey, they had allegedly taken money from famed New York gambler Arnold Rothstein to dump the Series. Gandil and Boston gambler Sport Sullivan hatched the plot, Rothstein bankrolled it, and the Sox dropped the Series.

There were signed confessions, retracted confessions, stolen evidence, and other mischief, and in the end the eight players were acquitted on August 2, 1921. But that didn't matter to Landis, nor did the fact that Jackson and Weaver actually played quite well in the Series, as a day later the new commissioner barred all eight for life, knotting them together forever in the lore of sports.

The eight will also be tied together for what was lost—and what happened to the Sox.

The greatest loss was Jackson, who was comparable to Ty Cobb and Tris Speaker and batting .356 when his career ended. Though he was 34 when he was banned, Jackson still had a few great years left to burnish his reputation as one of baseball's early legends.

"He batted against spitballs, shineballs, emeryballs, and all the other trick deliveries," Cobb said of Jackson. "He never figured anything out or studied anything with the same scientific approach I gave it. He just swung. If he'd ever had any knowledge of batting, his average would have been phenomenal. . . . He seemed content to just punch the ball, and I can still see those line drives whistling to the far precincts. Joe Jackson hit the ball harder than any man ever to play baseball."

Without Jackson and the rest of the eight (Weaver maintained his innocence until his death), the Sox's fortunes plummeted. A team that won the 1917 World Series, the AL pennant in 1919, and 96 games in 1920 finished 62–92 in 1921. The Sox had only two more winning seasons in the 1920s. And while the sport boomed during the 1920s as Babe Ruth and the Yankees became national icons, the White Sox foundered and puttered along, trying to wash off the stain of the 1919 team.

▲ Had he not been banned, Joe Jackson's legacy might have been comparable to that of Ty Cobb or Tris Speaker.

If that team had stayed together, who knows what would have happened? Maybe the Sox would have challenged the Yankees during the 1920s and forged a true Chicago–New York baseball rivalry. The 1920s Sox might not have beaten the Yankees every year, but another couple of pennants could have changed the landscape nationally while the crosstown Cubs went through their first down period.

Most important, it took until the 1950s and the Go-Go era for the team to recover. If they ever truly did.

They Never Stopped Believin'

It's not rare for a team to talk about adopting an identity. It's much rarer when teams actually follow through and turn that identity into something truly special.

The 2005 White Sox did just that.

Despite an 83-win 2004 season and an active offseason that saw Jermaine Dye, Scott Podsednik, Bobby Jenks, Tadahito Iguchi, and A.J. Pierzynski come to US Cellular Field, not much was expected of second-year manager Ozzie Guillen and the 2005 Sox. But it quickly became apparent that these Sox were different.

They lived up to the slogan "Win. Or Die Trying." Center fielder Aaron Rowand made a name for himself jumping into walls, Joe Crede gobbled everything up at third base, Juan Uribe and Iguchi caught everything up the middle, Podsednik caused problems at the top of the order, and Dye, Everett, and Paul Konerko (and briefly Frank Thomas) provided the thump. And the pitching made any offense stand up. Jose Contreras, a bust for the Yankees, became a dominant starter, Mark Buehrle grew into a cult hero and staff leader, Jon Garland (who was swiped from the Cubs in 1998) matured, and Freddy Garcia had one of his best seasons. Meanwhile, Jenks took over as closer by late summer and added even more heat to a lethal bullpen.

It was a dream team off to a dream start, and it led the AL Central by 15 games on August 1. And then . . . oh, no.

One bad loss after another. Cleveland kept coming and coming, and the Sox were staggering. The lead kept dwindling until September 22, when the Indians were just a game and a half behind.

"Whether the Sox go on to finish the biggest regular-season fold in baseball history or somehow do a backdoor slider into the playoffs, it should be obvious now that the rampaging Indians are a much better team and are worthier of the American League Central title," Jay Mariotti wrote in the *Chicago Sun-Times*.

The Sox recovered to win eight of their final 10 games and hold off the Indians, but people weren't exactly optimistic about their chances in the playoffs. Chicago won 99 games overall, but first up in the playoffs were the defending-champion, curse-busting Boston Red Sox, who surely would overwhelm the sagging White Sox.

Uh, no. And that's when the opportunism that made the 2005 Sox a team for the ages began to really take hold. Game 1 against Boston was a 14–2 White Sox win. Game 2 was the first playoff moment in which these Sox showed they had something else. With the White Sox down 4–2 in the fifth, Uribe appeared to hit into an inning-ending double play, but the ball went through Tony Graffanino's legs. Two batters later, Iguchi homered off David Wells to give the Sox a 5–4 lead they held the rest of the night. In Game 3, the Sox led 4–3 in the sixth inning, but Damaso Marte loaded the bases with no outs and in came Orlando "El Duque" Hernandez. Known for coming through in the playoffs with the Yankees, Hernandez got two pop-ups and then struck out Johnny Damon to end the threat. Three innings later, the Sox were in the AL Championship Series.

And that's when things really got going.

The Angels won Game 1 and were poised to take Game 2 to extra innings when Pierzynski struck out to end the ninth. But Pierzynski ran to first even though it looked as if catcher Josh Paul caught strike three cleanly. The umpires agreed with Pierzynski that the ball hit the ground before going into Paul's glove and kept him at first. Break or not, the Sox took advantage when Crede doubled in pinch-runner Pablo Ozuna for the winning run.

"Do we feel lucky? No," Pierzynski said. "Did they feel lucky when they won last night?"

The next three games weren't about luck. They were about the Sox's rotation. After Buehrle went the distance in Game 2, Garland did the same in a Game 3 win, Garcia matched that in Game 4, and Contreras wrapped up the Sox's first pennant since 1959 with a complete game of his own.

"Those guys were the horses, and I was just along for the ride," ALCS MVP Konerko said of the rotation. "Really, we all were."

The ride was becoming legendary. Journey's "Don't Stop Believin'" had become the team's theme song and an anthem for fans everywhere. Guillen, thanks to his big mouth and managing acumen, was becoming a sensation, and the previously anonymous White Sox were becoming stars. Now they needed only to beat the Astros to become champions.

Game 1 was a routine 5–3 win, capped off by Jenks blowing away the Astros in the ninth inning. Game 2 was more Sox magic. Konerko's grand slam in the seventh vaulted the Sox to a 6–4 lead and came one batter after Dye was ruled to have been hit by a pitch, though replays showed the ball hit his bat. Jenks coughed up two runs to tie the score in

BELIEVE! The Sox celebrate their 2005 World Series victory after shutting out the Astros 1–0 in Game 4 to complete the sweep.

the ninth, but Podsednik, whose only Sox homer came in the AL Division Series against Boston, sent everybody home with a drive over the fence in right-center.

The Sox were two wins away. They had to wait a long time for the third, but it came in the 14th inning when Geoff Blum, the team's lone acquisition before the trade deadline, homered down the right-field line. Buehrle, who allegedly had a beer earlier in the night, saved the game. The next night, the Sox made history thanks to Series MVP Dye's go-ahead single, Uribe's catch of a pop-up in the first row of seats for the second out of the ninth, and finally Uribe throwing out Orlando Palmeiro at first for the Sox's championship.

The Sox never did stop believing. And nobody will forget them.

The Most Innovative Team in Baseball

Baseball is a sport that can become entrenched in habits. There are times when the game—as wonderful as it is—gets stuck in a rut and simply sticks too close to its past and doesn't move into the future. The White Sox have never been guilty of this.

Throughout their illustrious history, the Sox have been one of baseball's creative forces. Sure, that's partly because they were owned twice by Bill Veeck, but there has always been a vibe of innovation around the South Siders. It's a franchise that has tried different things at different times. Ideas such as Disco Demolition Night or the late-1970s collared uniforms that briefly included shorts are two that never should've been tried.

But failure can be the cost of trying something different, and the Sox have never shied away from standing out.

Here are three lasting inventions the Sox pioneered that have influenced not just baseball but sports as a whole.

The Exploding Scoreboard

For the first 60 years of the 20th century, pretty much every scoreboard was the same. They were staid objects that told you the score and the count, and gave you updates on what was happening in other games around the league. Not much else.

Then, as the story goes, Veeck saw the Jimmy Cagney movie *The Time of Your Life* and was inspired by the brightly lit pinball machine Cagney's character played.

Veeck, ever the innovator, took that visual and expanded it for the scoreboard at Comiskey Park. Complete with sounds, lights, patterns, and fireworks, the scoreboard "exploded" for the first time on May 1, 1960, when outfielder Al Smith homered.

Other than coming up with a new way to entertain fans, Veeck also started the scoreboard arms race that exists to this day. Now, it's not enough to just tell people the score. Videoboards are getting bigger and bigger, with clearer screens and more bells and whistles. That all dates back to Veeck.

Names on Uniforms

Veeck must've been inspired by the team's 1959 AL pennant, because the exploding scoreboard wasn't his only eureka moment in 1960.

Until adopting their current look in 1990, the Sox were never known for sticking with one for long. They had different colors and logos and designs, but nothing really lasted. Yet the change they made in 1960, adding player names to the back of the road uniforms, didn't just last; it soon became the norm in all major sports.

Veeck made the change because he thought fans watching games in person should know a player's name, like those watching on TV who saw the names projected on the screen. But this wasn't a popular move with the players at first.

"All we really need now are our telephone numbers on our uniforms, and we'll have as much privacy as goldfish," one said.

FOUR KEY MOVES
THAT SHAPED THE SOX

Like all teams, the Sox have made choices that didn't work out—trading Sammy Sosa to the Cubs was a gaffe and firing Tony LaRussa was inexplicable—but they've also had shrewd decisions that affected not just the team on the field, but its culture away from the game.

The Trade for Fox

In 1949, the White Sox were going nowhere fast. So on October 19, they sent catcher Joe Tipton to the Athletics for Nellie Fox. All you have to know about this deal is that Tipton appeared in 159 games for the A's over three seasons and was out of baseball by 1954. Fox, meanwhile, went on to have a Hall of Fame career, playing in 2,115 games for the Sox and making 12 All-Star teams. The deal itself was strong, but it set the tone for a decade of great Sox baseball and how they would play the game.

Veeck Sells and Buys and Sells

Bill Veeck was a showman, an iconoclast, and a genuine human being, but he never stayed in one place for long. In 1959, he bought the Sox and in three years won a pennant, installed the exploding scoreboard, and put names on the back of the uniforms. But he also had no patience for young players and oversaw deals to send away many top prospects. The Allyns, who bought

That player's objections didn't come to pass. The Sox added names to the back of their home uniforms in 1961, and now only the Yankees, Red Sox, and Giants wear non-throwback home uniforms that don't have player names on the back. The White Sox have tried other uniform innovations that didn't pan out—such as the shorts the team wore for three games in 1976—but this one certainly did.

the team in 1961, went on to install an artificial-turf infield at Comiskey and changed its name to Sox Park, and the team almost moved multiple times. In 1975, Veeck bought the Sox back and made sure they stayed at renamed Comiskey. But by 1980, after an up-and-down few years, Veeck sold to Jerry Reinsdorf and Eddie Einhorn. Veeck wasn't a total success with the Sox, but he bought when they needed him and sold when the time was right. Twice.

Trade for Guillen

A seven-player trade in 1984 helped define the next 25 years of White Sox baseball. Shortstop Ozzie Guillen was a sparkplug on the field and helped the Sox to the 1993 AL West title. In the fall of 2003, Guillen was back to manage the team after the White Sox tired of laid-back Jerry Manuel. Guillen was the opposite, pushing the team every day with his passion and his mouth. He also knew the game as well as anybody, and it showed as he deftly managed the 2005 Sox to their great triumph. Unfortunately, the parts of Guillen people loved also led to him wearing out his welcome. In 2011, he was allowed to leave for the Miami Marlins.

Changing Uniform Colors

Before 1990, the Sox had no true visual identity, having never settled on a color scheme or logo. That changed in 1990, when the team unveiled a silver-and-black uniform with the stylized Sox logo that first appeared in 1950. It was an identity that transcended sports and crossed over to pop culture. They had a new slogan (Good Guys Wear Black), and the white pinstripe home uniforms and gray roads with the cursive Chicago are still worn to this day. Don't underestimate how important this change was. The Sox never had a look. Now they had one, and they have no reason to ever change again.

Turn Back the Clock

The 1990 season was one of the most fun in White Sox history. A young team not expected to do much challenged the powerhouse Oakland Athletics deep into September and finished second in the AL West with a record of 94–68.

The year was also a six-month celebration of Comiskey Park, which was hosting its 81st and final season of baseball before it was torn down and the Sox moved across the street to their new building. On July 11, 1990, the Sox hosted Turn Back the Clock Day at Old Comiskey during which players wore versions of the 1917 uniforms, the game featured a hand-operated scoreboard, and the public-address system was silenced for the day.

"We should wear these all year—they're better than what we've got now," shortstop Ozzie Guillen said in 1990. "Look at all the uniforms in the All-Star Game and who had the ugliest one? The White Sox."

Ugliness of Chicago's late-1980s uniforms aside, the Turn Back the Clock Day promotion was the first of its kind. Soon, other teams jumped on the bandwagon to honor past teams and eras.

The day also brought throwback uniforms into people's brains. It seems as if every team now rocks a throwback at least once a season, and fans everywhere buy them at exorbitant prices.

NICE LOOK? Rich "Goose" Gossage and the White Sox wore shorts as their official uniform for three memorable games in 1976.

CHICAGO WHITE SOX
MOUNT RUSHMORE

Luis Aparicio (1956–1962, 1968–1970), Nellie Fox (1950–1963)

No two players personified the Go-Go style more than shortstop Aparicio and second baseman Fox. Fox's arrival before the 1950 season in a trade with the Athletics was the first sign of a new future for the Sox. He made an immediate impact for the up-and-coming team, making the All-Star team for the first time in 1951 and emerging as one of the sport's best second basemen.

Fox got his best double-play partner in 1956 when Aparicio was called up to Chicago. Aparicio became the first Latin American player to win Rookie of the Year, and by 1958 he was the AL's starter in the All-Star Game.

Everything came together for the Go-Go Sox in 1959. The Yankees went only 79–75, and the Sox won the pennant by five games over Cleveland. Fox won the MVP, and Aparicio finished second but won a Gold Glove.

Luke Appling (1930–1943, 1945–1950)

The time between the Black Sox and the Go-Go era of the 1950s was generally a bleak one for the White Sox. They never contended for much and struggled to stay in the top half of the AL standings. One reason for Sox fans to buy tickets was "Old Aches and Pains" Luke Appling, a sweet-swinging shortstop with a knack for finding ways to collect base hits.

Appling was an endearing figure who could hit. He had nine straight .300 seasons, and his career reached its peak in 1936 when he hit .388 and drove in 128 runs. He was the first AL shortstop to win the batting title and was an All-Star for the first time. Along with Hall of Fame pitcher Ted Lyons, Appling led a mini renaissance for the Sox in the late 1930s. The 1936 team went 81–70, the 1937 Sox finished a strong third in the AL with 86 victories, and the 1939 team went 85–69 before another strong 82-win season in 1940.

Appling did have one final moment in the spotlight during a July 19, 1982, old-timers game when the 75-year-old hit a home run off Warren Spahn.

Carlton Fisk (1981–1993)

Fisk was the rock of the Sox for almost 13 seasons and gave the team a hard-working identity. A native New Englander, Fisk left Boston in free agency before the 1981 season and got revenge almost immediately. On April 10 at Fenway Park, he hit a go-ahead, three-run homer in the eighth inning of a 5–3 White Sox win. He was the first major signing by new White Sox owners Jerry Reinsdorf and Eddie Einhorn, sending a signal to baseball that the Sox were ready to compete again after the Bill Veeck era.

Two years later, the Sox were big winners. With Fisk behind the plate and finishing third in MVP voting, the Winning Ugly Sox claimed 99 victories and the AL West title for their first playoff appearance in 24 years.

Two years later, the 37-year-old Fisk hit 37 homers, and in 1993, he set the record for most games caught by a catcher six days before an unceremonious release ended his career.

Frank Thomas (1990–2005)

The Big Hurt never became a national household name, but he was a great hitter and scary presence in the Sox lineup.

Almost from the moment he came up in 1990, Thomas was a monster. He hit .318 with 32 homers in his first full season, and in 1993 he led the Sox to a division title and won the first of two straight AL MVP Awards. His 1994 season is one of the great what-ifs in baseball, as he was hitting .353 with 38 home runs and had a chance to both surpass Roger Maris and win a Triple Crown when the strike hit in mid-August.

▶ Frank Thomas

Thomas's sheer size and power, which came without the help of performance-enhancing drugs, was supplemented by a keen batting eye. He won a batting title in 1997 and made a strong MVP case in 2000 when the Sox won the AL Central. Unfortunately, Thomas was hurt for much of 2005 and could only watch as the Sox finally won the World Series.

CHICAGO WHITE SOX
BEST OF THE REST

Dick Allen (1972–1974)

Allen spent only three seasons with the Sox, but they were three big ones. The first baseman's finest was 1972, when he hit 37 homers, drove in 113 runs, and kept the Sox within shouting distance of the powerful Athletics for most of the season, winning the AL MVP Award.

Mark Buehrle (2000–2011)

Buehrle worked fast and was a fan favorite because of his attitude and work ethic on the mound. A 38th-round pick, Buehrle became one of the most accomplished figures in Sox history. He threw a perfect game and a no-hitter and was a key part of the 2005 World Series champions.

Eddie Collins (1915–1926)

Collins rose to prominence with the Philadelphia Athletics and was sold to Charles Comiskey and the Sox before the 1915 season, just as the team was ready to contend. Collins was the starting second baseman on the 1917 team that won the World Series and the 1919 team that won the AL pennant, later becoming a player-manager from 1924 through 1926.

Red Faber (1914–1933)

Faber was a key part of the 1917 rotation but missed the 1919 World Series because of injury. It's fair to wonder how history could've changed if this Hall of Famer had pitched in the fateful Series.

Ozzie Guillen (1985–1997, player, 2004–2011, manager)

You cannot write the history of the White Sox without Guillen. The 1985 AL Rookie of the Year played 13 seasons in Chicago before returning to manage in 2004. One World Series title, two playoff berths, and countless controversies later, Guillen's legacy will live on forever.

Joe Jackson (1915–1920)

Shoeless Joe was the greatest tragedy of the 1919 Black Sox. He had standout and memorable teammates, but Jackson was the best of the lot. If not for the scandal, he would easily be one of the 10 greatest hitters of the 20th century and perhaps the greatest White Sox player of all time.

Paul Konerko (1999–2014)

His grand slam in the seventh inning of Game 2 of the 2005 World Series will go down in baseball lore, but the power-hitting first baseman was much more than that one moment. Konerko hit 432 home runs and drove in 1,383 runs during his 16 years on the South Side.

Ted Lyons (1923–1942, 1946, player, 1946–1948, manager)

Lyons, a pitcher, missed three seasons to serve in World War II and spent his last three seasons in Chicago as a player-manager and then manager. Lyons won all 260 games of his career with the White Sox and was one of the team's few bright spots between the Black Sox and the 1950s.

Minnie Minoso (1951–1957, 1960–1961, 1964, 1976, 1980)

Minoso was Chicago's first black player and a truly wonderful ambassador for the team until his passing in 2015. He started the team's great tradition of Cuban players and built relationships with stars such as Jose Abreu and Alexei Ramirez.

Ray Schalk (1912–1928)

Schalk was the catcher for the White Sox's 1917 World Series champion and was the backstop for the infamous 1919 team. Never implicated in the Black Sox scandal, Schalk was elected to the Hall of Fame in 1955.

Ed Walsh (1904–1916)

The Sox have been built around great pitching, and Walsh was their first true ace. He averaged 24 victories from 1906 through 1912 and was the best pitcher on the 1906 team, which upset the Cubs to win the World Series.

▶ Minnie Minoso

CHAPTER 6
THE COLLEGES

Fans in Chicago often look outward for their college sports and cheer for Notre Dame and Illinois. But for those loyal to more distant programs, they can risk missing out on some of the unique programs right in the Chicagoland area, whether that's Division I programs such as Northwestern, DePaul, and Loyola, or the many smaller schools with their own unique fan bases and traditions.

Northwestern owns the greatest local standing with its Big Ten affiliation, and at times the Wildcats have lived up to it. Excellence and NU football were mutually exclusive until 1995, and nobody expected much from the Wildcats entering that season. They had been a "respectable" 3–7–1 in 1994, but few thought they could do anything beyond maybe finishing with five wins in 1995. Game 1 at Notre Dame was supposed to be a loss, but with a defense led by linebacker Pat Fitzgerald and an offense powered by running back

◀ No one could have expected the magical season cornerback Chris Martin and the Northwestern Wildcats put together in 1995.

Darnell Autry, Northwestern stunned the Irish and the nation with a 17–15 win. Up next was Miami of Ohio in Evanston, and the Wildcats blew a big lead and lost 30–28.

For sure, that meant the Wildcats were back to their old ways, right? Not a chance.

They recovered to rout Air Force and Indiana before visiting No. 7 Michigan. Somehow, NU pulled out a 19–13 win at soggy Michigan Stadium, and all of a sudden the Wildcats were a national story.

Minnesota and Wisconsin were vanquished, Illinois was repelled late, and on November 4, the Wildcats welcomed Joe Paterno and Penn State to Dyche Stadium. With Keith Jackson on the call, NU won 21–10 and the talk of a Rose Bowl was becoming real. Autry was a Heisman candidate and on the cover of *Sports Illustrated*, and Barnett was earning praise for his coaching. The regular season ended with a victory at Purdue, and when Ohio State lost at Michigan a week later, the 10–1 (8–0 in conference) Wildcats were headed to Pasadena, California, to face Southern California in the Rose Bowl.

Really. The Wildcats were celebrities. Northwestern football was a national story. OK, the story ended with a 41–32 loss to USC, but the legacy of that season will never be tarnished.

Northwestern now markets itself as "Chicago's Big Ten Team," and the Wildcats' recent upswing helps the promotional push. Under Fitzgerald, the team's head coach since 2006, the Wildcats are a stable and dependably competent football team. As for men's basketball, coach Chris Collins led NU to its first NCAA Tournament in school history in 2017, perhaps setting the stage for the program to mature into a conference contender. But, inarguably, the most successful team at Northwestern is the women's lacrosse program.

HISTORIC Loyola takes on Mississippi State in the 1963 Sweet 16 at Jenison Field House in East Lansing, Michigan.

Under coach Kelly Amonte Hiller, NU in 2005 began a streak of seven national titles in eight years and set a standard for excellence that's hard to top.

Speaking of historic, one of Chicago's Catholic universities owns a national title, and that's Loyola—though few remember it. Long before Sister Jean and the Ramblers made their unlikely run to the 2018 Final Four as an 11 seed, the Ramblers won the 1963 national championship. It's an accomplishment that has fallen through the cracks of Chicago sports lore. Maybe it's because the Bears won the NFL championship later that year, or maybe it's because of how small a school Loyola is. Whatever the reason, the Ramblers had a historic and important season.

Three years before Texas Western started an all-black lineup against Kentucky, coach George Ireland routinely started four black players at the same time.

"We were spit on in Houston," Ron Miller said. "I remember that the ball went out of bounds. I go to pick it up, and I see this lady sitting there, dressed really nice, and she looks at me. And then she uttered a racial slur."

The Ramblers were also part of a historic moment on March 15 against Mississippi State in the second round of the tournament. At that time, teams from Mississippi weren't allowed to play integrated opponents, and the Bulldogs had to violate an injunction to play. The moment isn't as well known as what Texas Western did three years later in Maryland, but it still resonates.

What the Ramblers did on the court also resonates. They went 29–2 and upset two-time defending champion Cincinnati 60–58 to win the title, the only one for an Illinois school. Despite struggling from the floor, the Ramblers got the game to overtime and had a chance to win. But instead of shooting, All-American Jerry Harkness passed to Les Hunter, whose shot clanged off the rim but was rebounded by Vic Rouse, who scored the winning basket.

Unlike Loyola, DePaul's golden era of excellence in the late 1970s and 1980s is still fondly remembered. That was a great time to be a DePaul Blue Demons men's basketball fan. The players were charismatic, the coach was lovable, the program was cool, and the team was really good. The best it got was in 1979, when coach Ray Meyer and star Mark Aguirre led the Blue Demons to the Final Four.

Entering the NCAA Tournament 21–5, DePaul reeled off wins over USC and rival Marquette, and then beat UCLA 95–91 to reach the school's second Final Four. Waiting was Indiana State and a gawky forward named Larry Bird. Despite Aguirre and Gary Garland scoring 19 points apiece, Bird had 35 and the Demons' run was over after a 76–74 loss.

"It's tough," Meyer said. "We laughed a lot all year; now we cry a little. . . . But I can't be depressed now. Not when we played a basketball game. We didn't lose our lives. We didn't lose a war. . . . I'm just sorry we couldn't win for all the fans back in Chicago."

Beyond Chicago

For as much as the Chicago-area colleges have to offer, the big players still come from just outside the city. That starts with the Notre Dame Fighting Irish.

Somehow, the tiny Catholic school in South Bend, Indiana, has built itself into one of the finest all-around athletics departments in the nation, having won national titles in three women's sports (basketball, fencing, soccer) and five men's sports (cross country, fencing, golf, soccer, tennis), plus the 11 championships claimed by the Fighting Irish football team.

From Knute Rockne to Rudy Ruettiger, George "The Gipper" Gipp to Lou Holtz, the Four Horsemen to Tony Rice, and Frank Leahy and Ara Parseghian to Dan Devine, the Irish have risen to become more than a football team. They're a way of life for fans all over the country (they have their own national TV deal!) and play their home games just two hours from Chicago.

No school has more lore than Notre Dame, and no Notre Dame moment is more iconic than Rockne's famous "Win one for the Gipper" speech he gave in 1928. The story began in 1920, when Irish star Gipp died of strep throat and reportedly told Rockne on his deathbed: "I've got to go, Rock. It's all right. I'm not afraid. Some time, Rock, when the team is up against it, when things are wrong and the breaks are beating the boys, ask them to go in there with all they've got and win just one for the Gipper. I don't know where I'll be then, Rock. But I'll know about it, and I'll be happy."

Eight years later, at halftime of the Irish's November 10, 1928, game against Army, Rockne told Gipp's story. With the score tied at halftime, the Irish upset Army 12–6. In 1940, the story was the basis of the movie *Knute Rockne, All American* starring future president Ronald Reagan as Gipp.

A couple of hours south of Chicago is the University of Illinois. As the alma mater of Dick Butkus, Red Grange, and George Halas, no university has had more of an impact on the Bears than the U of I. Halas brought his alma mater's colors to the Bears, and Butkus and Grange became defining players in Chicago. The program itself has had patches of success, winning more than a dozen Big Ten titles and three Rose Bowls. The men's basketball team has long been the most important program in Champaign, and the success of the hoops team has gone a long way toward defining the athletics department. The 2005 team came within a whisker of a national title, and the Flyin' Illini flew to the Final Four in 1989, but the team arguably reached its greatest heights in the early 1950s, making the Final Four three times between 1949 and 1952 under Harry Combes.

That 2004–05 Fighting Illini team didn't win the national championship, but there won't be a more perfect college basketball team assembled for some time. That season also showed what kind of Illini city Chicago can be.

In his second year, coach Bruce Weber took the players left by former coach Bill Self and turned them into a cohesive unit. The backcourt featured Deron Williams and Dee Brown. James Augustine and Roger Powell Jr. brought toughness up front. And the team started to win and win and win, starting 29–0 before losing its regular-season finale at Ohio State. No matter, the Illini breezed to the Big Ten tournament title at the United Center and entered the NCAA Tournament as the nation's No. 1 team.

After three relatively easy wins, Illinois trailed Arizona by 15 points in the regional final in Rosemont, Illinois. But Williams got hot, and the Illini rallied for a raucous 90–89 win and a trip to the Final Four in St. Louis.

▲ Dee Brown and the Illini capped off a memorable 2005 season with a run to the final.

"It's really hard to explain the feeling during that stretch," Augustine said. "When you're in Assembly Hall, the place explodes, and everything's shaking. It's so loud, and you can't think. This whole emotion was completely different. We were coming back, people were screaming. There was so much emotion that it was almost like an out-of-body experience."

The Illini knocked off Louisville 72–57 in the national semifinal, but North Carolina and its talented roster were too much, ending Illinois's season with a 75–70 decision in the national championship game.

Illinois isn't the only outstate school to leave its mark. Even Northern Illinois in DeKalb has had its share of moments, notably the 2012 team making the Orange Bowl. And if they're not cheering on one of the local teams, college sports fans are still all over Chicago. Whether they're packing the sports bars on Saturdays, filling United Center for Big Ten men's basketball tournaments, or suffering through freezing temperatures to watch outdoor hockey at Soldier Field, fans are always there. Chicago is far from just a pro sports city.

The Ghosts of Hyde Park

When you walk around the University of Chicago campus today, you see few signs that this was once the home of an early dynasty in college football. The university lives up to its austere reputation: The buildings are dark and foreboding, and there's a vibe of ultra-serious intellectualism, one that wouldn't seem conducive to rooting for a major football team every Saturday. But once upon a time, the Maroons ruled the Big Ten and helped create modern college football.

With the Midway Plaisance running through campus, the Maroons are the true and original Monsters of the Midway. Legend has it that in 1901 the Morgan Athletic Club bought faded old jerseys from the Maroons and said the shirts instead were cardinal red. That team turned into the Chicago (now Arizona) Cardinals.

In 1892, the university hired Amos Alonzo Stagg to run the nascent football team, and Stagg's impact was felt quickly. The Maroons became a power in what turned into the Big Ten, winning the first of their seven conference titles in 1899 to go with claimed national championships in 1905 and 1913.

Stagg was an innovator, for better and for worse. He pioneered the use of tackling dummies, huddling, varsity letters, and early versions of postseason bowls. He also pioneered some aspects of college football that the sport probably wishes he hadn't: steering players to professors who were sympathetic to football, shady recruiting tactics, and even some under-the-table compensation.

Under Stagg, the Maroons played on campus and built intense rivalries with Michigan and Northwestern. If the Maroons weren't the defining power of college football in that era, they were in the conversation. The aptly named Stagg Field held more than 50,000 fans and was the heartbeat of the campus.

Yet, by the mid-1920s, the program's decline had begun.

The school struggled to keep up with the bigger universities in the conference. Compounding the matter, the school's priority shifted away from major varsity athletics and more toward academics. The 1929 team went a respectable 7–3 under Stagg, but that season was the beginning of the end.

Nineteen twenty-nine was not only the final winning season for the Maroons but also the year Robert Maynard Hutchins became president of the university. Hutchins implemented sweeping changes to the school and was no fan of major football being played on a college campus.

"The whole apparatus of football, fraternities, and fun is a means by which education is made palatable to those who have no business in it," Hutchins said.

He forced Stagg out after the 1932 season and replaced him with future Stanford coach and T-formation innovator Clark Shaughnessy. But Shaughnessy was powerless to stop the decline, even though the 1935 team featured halfback Jay Berwanger, who won a trophy from the Downtown Athletic Club to honor the best player east of the Mississippi River.

That award later became the Heisman Trophy, giving the Maroons the first winner of the prestigious crown.

Unfortunately for the few fans of Maroons football who remained, that was the last hurrah. The school increasingly had no business in major sports, and after the 1939 season the university pulled the plug on football. In 1946, it dropped out of the Big Ten.

"The game hampered the university's efforts to become the kind of institution it aspired to be," Hutchins said.

Today, the Maroons play football, but the Division III program draws little interest from anybody outside of the school. The team plays at Stagg Field, but the facility is part of a multipurpose venue that would look more appropriate for a high school team. The old Stagg Field was torn down in 1957 and replaced by a library.

Perhaps fittingly, the legacy of the stadium lives on, as under the west bleachers on December 2, 1942, University of Chicago physicist Enrico Fermi and his team created the first man-made nuclear chain reaction.

▲ The University of Chicago's Jay Berwanger strikes the Heisman pose.

THE FIVE DEFINING COACHES
IN CHICAGO-AREA COLLEGES

College sports are the kingdom of coaches. The schools in the Chicago area have been led by some of college sports' greatest leaders.

5. Kelly Amonte Hiller, Northwestern (2002–)

Under Amonte Hiller, the Northwestern women's lacrosse team became a dynasty, winning seven national championships in eight years and setting a standard for the sport. No Midwestern team had won even one title in the sport before the Wildcats.

4. Amos Alonzo Stagg, University of Chicago (1892–1932)

Stagg was a football innovator and contributed to the birth of the T formation, which was the first modern offense. He won two national titles at the University of Chicago and left the school with a 244–111–27 record.

3. Ara Parseghian, Northwestern (1956–1963), Notre Dame (1964–1974)

Parseghian's 1959 Northwestern football team spent six weeks with the No. 2 ranking, and in 1962 the Wildcats reached the top of the Associated Press poll after beating Ohio State and Notre Dame. However, Parseghian and athletics director Stu Holcomb clashed, and Parseghian wasn't offered a new contract after 1963. Instead, Parseghian landed at Notre Dame, where he led the Irish to two national titles and left as one of that school's greatest coaches.

2. Knute Rockne, Notre Dame (1918–1930)

Rockne was hired in 1918 and coached the Irish football team for 13 seasons. He won three national titles and went 105–12–5 before dying in a plane crash in March 1931. The lore of the Irish began with Rockne, who coached the Four Horsemen and delivered the fabled 1928 "Win one for the Gipper" speech.

1. Ray Meyer, DePaul (1942–1984)

A Chicago native and a Notre Dame alum, Meyer took over the Blue Demons men's basketball team in 1942 and had instant success. He recruited George Mikan and took DePaul to a Final Four in 1943 and an NIT title in 1945. The program had its ups and downs until the late 1970s, when the Demons exploded. They reached the 1979 Final Four and were the top basketball team in the city.

CHAPTER 7
CHICAGO AND THE OLYMPICS

Chicago can lay claim to being one of the most diverse sports markets in the country. But one thing it's missing is an Olympic Games.

Twice, in 1904 and then again in 2016, Chicago was in the queue to host the Games. And twice the city lost out because of factors well beyond its control. But maybe that shouldn't be Chicago's Olympic legacy. The city has produced some of the finest athletes to wear the red, white, and blue. There have been swimmers, gymnasts, figure skaters, and all-around athletes, and their accomplishments range from world records to the United States' first Olympic gold medals in men's team gymnastics and women's hockey.

Sure, it would be nice if Chicago had a legacy of hosting the Olympics. Then again, maybe it's everybody else's loss.

◀ Downers Grove native Cammi Granato celebrates after leading Team USA to the first Olympic women's hockey gold medal in 1998 in Nagano, Japan.

Maybe It's Not Meant to Be

The Columbian Exposition of 1893 was a smashing success for Chicago. Held on the South Side near the University of Chicago campus, the exposition brought visitors from all over the globe to the city that was only two decades removed from the Great Chicago Fire. The architecture was stunning, the ships in Lake Michigan gorgeous, and the city proved it could host a big event under the most challenging conditions.

Because of that success, the fledgling International Olympic Committee awarded the 1904 Games to Chicago. These Games would be the third overall, and the first to be held on US soil. Except St. Louis took them.

St. Louis, then the country's fourth-largest city (Chicago was second), was planning to host the 1903 World's Fair but pushed the event back to 1904. It also took aim at hosting a major athletic event at the same time. Baron Pierre de Coubertin, the founder and then-president of the IOC, chose to hand the Olympic Games to St. Louis. It did not go well.

The Games lasted four and a half months and were secondary to the World's Fair. Only 12 nations competed, and only 62 athletes from outside North America made it to the event. The marathon, held in the middle of a typically nasty St. Louis summer, was a symbol of the shambolic Games. New Yorker Frederick Lorz was originally declared the winner, though he was disqualified when officials learned he rode at least 10 miles in a car.

Then the actual winner, a Massachusetts clown—literally—named Thomas Hicks, finished only because he downed a regimen of strychnine sulfate and brandy, and still he almost died at the stadium.

Maybe then it's good that Chicago doesn't have that black mark on its record. The 1904 Games are generally considered a disaster, and St. Louis will likely never get another chance at hosting.

What happened in 2009, however, still stings.

Though Chicago had never hosted the Games, it looked like a perfect fit. With major sports teams and major universities and a slew of arenas, there were plenty of ready-made facilities. Under Mayor Richard M. Daley, Chicago had modernized itself with building

▲ With her famous bobbed hairstyle and signature camel spin, Chicago-born Dorothy Hamill won the 1976 Olympic women's figure skating gold medal.

projects and a new commitment to hosting major events. The city was also in need of new infrastructure and development, especially on the South Side. Plus, Chicago—a city as rabidly obsessed with sports as ever—is in the middle of the United States and close to multiple major airports. Simply put, Chicago had proven itself capable of hosting the world, so the city decided to bid for an opportunity to do just that in 2016.

At first, everything went well. The Chicago bid beat out Houston, Los Angeles, Philadelphia, and San Francisco to become the US Olympic Committee's candidate, and early indications were that Chicago's plan was impressive. The Games would be expensive, yes, but they would leave behind a legacy of new development and history for the city, particularly the new infrastructure for the relatively untouched South Side.

Understandably, the city was confident it would beat out Madrid, Spain; Rio de Janeiro, Brazil; and Tokyo, Japan, for the right to host the 2016 Games. The bid had a strong plan, general civic support (albeit with plenty of detractors), and celebrity backers such as basketball icon Michael Jordan, media darling Oprah Winfrey, and Barack Obama, who was still widely popular in his first year as president. Plus, the United States, whose corporations have long bankrolled the Olympic movement, hadn't hosted the Summer Games since 1996 in Atlanta. We were due.

The big day was October 2, 2009, in Copenhagen, Denmark.

Both President Obama, who had adopted Chicago as his hometown, and First Lady Michelle Obama spoke as part of the US delegation's final pitch. The First Lady, who was raised on the South Side, left the strongest impression with her impassioned speech.

"Sports were a gift I shared with my dad, especially the Olympic Games," she said. "Some of my best memories are sitting on my dad's lap, cheering on Olga and Nadia, Carl Lewis and others for their brilliance and perfection. But I never dreamed that the Olympic flame might one day light up lives in my neighborhood. But today, I can dream, and I

SWIM STAR Chicago native and butterfly specialist Pablo Morales won his first three medals, including a gold, at the 1984 Olympics in Los Angeles.

am dreaming of an Olympic and Paralympic Games in Chicago that will light up lives in neighborhoods all across America and all across the world."

Added Daley, "We want to share our city with the world."

After the presentation, everyone was feeling good. "I think Chicago could not have made a better presentation," President Obama said.

All that was left was the vote. The first round of voting included 94 votes, and one bid would be eliminated. IOC president Jacques Rogge announced the first elimination.

"The city of Chicago, having obtained the least number of votes, will not participate in the next round," Rogge read.

Stunning. Absolutely stunning.

Whether you were for or against the Games coming to Chicago, the city's civic pride was wounded. It was rejected by the international crowd and slapped down a peg. Its chance to show off in front of the world was gone.

> "I never dreamed that the Olympic flame might one day light up lives in my neighborhood. But today, I can dream, and I am dreaming of an Olympic and Paralympic Games in Chicago that will light up lives in neighborhoods all across America and all across the world."
>
> - Michelle *OBAMA*
> FIRST LADY AND CHICAGO NATIVE PITCHING THE CHICAGO OLYMPIC BID TO THE IOC IN 2009

Today, nobody knows for sure why Chicago was the first city eliminated. Was there an anti-American bias? Was the bid not as strong as Chicagoans perceived? Did it fail at the political game? Or did Rio, the eventual winner, engage in some underhandedness to claim the Games? Perhaps the likeliest reason was a revenue-sharing dispute between the IOC and the USOC at the time.

Whatever the reason, October 2, 2009, will go down in history as a dark day for Chicago, and a missed opportunity for everyone else.

"I have no doubt that it was the strongest bid possible, and I'm proud that I was able to come in and help make that case in person," President Obama said.

HE'S GOLDEN Naperville's Evan Lysacek broke a 22-year US men's drought when he won the figure skating gold medal in 2010 in Vancouver.

THE CHICAGO AREA'S
10 GREATEST OLYMPIANS

Bonnie Blair (1984, 1988, 1992, 1994)

As a speed skater, Blair won three consecutive Olympic gold medals in the 500-meter race and two in the 1,000. With six total medals—she also won a bronze in the 1,000—Blair is the most decorated US woman in the Winter Games. Raised in Champaign, Blair was a short-track world champion before leaving her mark on the 400-meter oval. In a career dotted with world records and world titles, Blair also won the 1992 Sullivan Award as the top amateur athlete in the United States and was named *Sports Illustrated*'s Sportswoman of the Year for 1994.

Bart Conner (1984)

Raised in Morton Grove and a graduate of Niles West High School, Conner won two gymnastics gold medals at the 1984 Games in Los Angeles. The US men won the Olympic team title for the first time, and Conner added a second gold medal in the parallel bars competition. He's also the winner of the parallel bars at the 1979 gymnastics world championships. Conner ended up marrying Romanian gymnastics legend Nadia Comaneci, whom he met in 1976 but didn't start dating until the early 1990s.

Shani Davis (2006, 2010, 2014, 2018)

A long-track speed skater, Davis was born and raised on Chicago's South Side and is one of the most decorated US competitors. The first black athlete to win gold in an individual event at a Winter Olympics, he has two Olympic gold medals, winning the 1,000 meters in 2006 and 2010, and 11 world championships titles, and he has set nine world records.

"When you're a world champion or an Olympic champion, you get this little thing on your back called a target," Davis said. "To go out there and win the 1,000 meters twice is truly amazing."

◀ Shani Davis

Cammi Granato (1998, 2002)

Among all the pioneers of women's hockey in the 1990s, Granato might have been the most impactful. Born in Downers Grove, Granato captained Team USA to the sport's first Olympic gold medal in 1998 in Nagano, Japan, and then she led the team to a silver medal four years later in Salt Lake City.

One of the first two women to be inducted into the Hockey Hall of Fame, Granato is also in the US Hockey Hall of Fame and has worked as a color commentator for international broadcasts. She's also the star of a family with no shortage of hockey acumen. Her brother Tony had a 13-year career in the NHL and coached both the Colorado Avalanche and the 2018 US Olympic men's team. Another brother, Don, was named an assistant coach with the Blackhawks in 2017. When it comes to hockey lore, though, it's Cammi Granato who left the greatest legacy.

"It's incredible what she's meant to hockey," network TV hockey analyst Mike Milbury said. "She's given hockey a profile (in the United States) more than good men's players have been able to."

Dorothy Hamill (1976)

Few athletes were as beloved as Hamill, who was born in Chicago. She reached the peak of her fame in 1976, winning gold in women's figure skating in both the Olympics and world championships. Hamill also became a fashion icon thanks to her hair and glasses, and created a signature move called the "Hamill Camel," which combined a camel spin and a sit spin. Later in life, Hamill has spoken openly about her depression, giving others hope and freedom to do the same.

"Skating is something that I loved since the very first time I put on skates," Hamill said. "I was eight years old, on a pond. It's something that got into my soul and my blood. It's my therapy."

Ethel Lackie (1924)

Lackie was one of the first great US swimmers. The Chicago native won two golds in swimming at the 1924 Games in Paris, France, individually in the 100-meter freestyle and as part of the 4x100 freestyle relay. The 100-meter freestyle team also included Gertrude Ederle, who became the first woman to swim across the English Channel. Their time of 4:58.8 set a world record.

THE CHICAGO AREA'S
10 GREATEST OLYMPIANS

Evan Lysacek (2006, 2010)

The area's strong history in figure skating continued when Lysacek, born in Chicago and raised in Naperville, won the 2010 Olympic gold medal. He had already won the 2009 world championship and continued to stake his claim as one of America's most accomplished skaters. He enjoyed multiple endorsements and used his name and fame for multiple charities.

"I saw that American flag go up, and I couldn't believe it was for me," Lysacek said after winning gold at the Vancouver Games. "I'm still in shock right now. I wasn't prepared for this. Going into this season, I never planned to win the gold medal."

Pablo Morales (1984, 1992)

The son of Cuban immigrants, Morales was born in Chicago and won gold medals in swimming at the 1984 and 1992 Games, despite missing out on the 1988 team. He took home gold twice in the 4x100 medley relay and also won individual gold in Barcelona, Spain, in the 100-meter butterfly after briefly retiring from the sport.

"There was a time where I didn't think it was going to happen," Morales said during the 1992 Barcelona Games, "and to come back kind of last moment to train for one more try to see it actually happen. The reality of it had an unreal quality to it. It had only been an idea up to that point."

Betty Robinson (1928, 1936)

The first US Olympic gold medalist in women's track and field, Robinson won the 100 meters in 1928 as a 16-year-old. Eight years later, she was part of Team USA's winning 4x100 relay in 1936, when the Americans upset the heavily favored Germans in Berlin. Robinson getting to Germany was impressive enough. The Riverdale native was in a plane crash in 1931, and when she was discovered, she was so seriously hurt that the person who found her thought she was dead and drove her to an undertaker. Robinson reportedly spent seven months in a coma, six months in a wheelchair, and two years learning to walk again, a saga that captured the attention of fans.

Johnny Weissmuller (1924, 1928)

Before he was Tarzan, Weissmuller and his family were ethnic German immigrants from Hungary who settled in Chicago. Weissmuller took up swimming after being diagnosed with polio.

"My doctor said I should take up some sort of exercise to build myself up," Weissmuller recalled. So he got into swimming, and, while working at the Illinois Athletic Club, was noticed by a coach who trained him. The rest is history. In 1924 in Paris, Weissmuller won three gold medals as a swimmer and a bronze medal in water polo. Four years later in Amsterdam, Netherlands, he added two more swimming gold medals while also playing on the water polo team. Weissmuller set more than 65 world records and is still considered one of the greatest swimmers of all time.

Thanks to his good looks and chiseled physique, Weissmuller caught the eye of movie producers, who cast him to play Tarzan. He played the role in one form or another more than 15 times and acted until 1976.

"It was like stealing," he said. "There was swimming in it, and I didn't have much to say. How can a guy climb trees, say 'Me Tarzan, you Jane,' and make a million?"

▶ Johnny Weissmuller

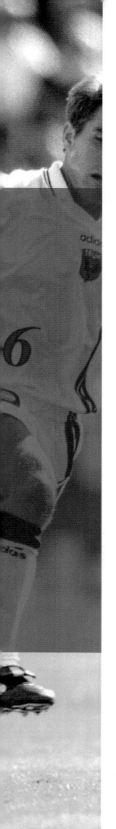

CHAPTER 8

BEYOND THE FIVE

The parking lots outside Toyota Park in suburban Bridgeview have a distinct pulse. Grills and barbecues are going, and that sweet smoky smell wafts through the air. Music from so many cultures and traditions can be heard, all somehow getting along in the same space. Kids and adults kick a soccer ball around, some not caring whether they hit a car or vice versa.

This is the scene before a Chicago Fire game. The team might not be a part of the big five, but the Fire are truly loved by their hardcore fans.

Founded in 1998, the Fire are still unique for their success as an expansion team. Playing at Soldier Field, the club got off on strong footing thanks to an impressive roster and a prescient hire for the first head coach. Before going on to international recognition with the US men's national team and becoming the first American to coach in a top-flight European league, Bob Bradley

◀ The Fire's Piotr Nowak races away from DC United defenders at the MLS Cup in 1998 at the Rose Bowl.

arrived in Chicago ready for his first big job. He had served on Bruce Arena's staff at DC United, which had won the first two MLS Cups, in 1996 and 1997.

The Fire didn't just finish above .500 or make the playoffs—they won the 1998 MLS Cup and US Open Cup titles *in their first season of existence.* Behind a stout defense that featured Goalkeeper of the Year Zach Thornton and Defender of the Year Lubos Kubik, as well as a midfield anchored by Polish veteran Piotr "Peter" Nowak, the Fire navigated their way through the MLS playoffs, finally getting through to the MLS Cup via shootout. Once there, they shut out DC United 2–0 in front of more than 50,000 fans at the Rose Bowl. That capped off the greatest season for an expansion team in any North American sport, and it's hard to see any team matching that feat anytime soon.

The Fire have had other high points, including the 2006 opening of Toyota Park, multiple US Open Cup wins, and memorable seasons with A-list players such as Mexico's Cuauhtemoc Blanco, Germany's Bastian Schweinsteiger, and the area's very own Brian McBride. However, the team is still in search of that elusive second league championship.

Yes, the Bears, Blackhawks, Bulls, Cubs, and White Sox take up most of Chicago's pro sports oxygen. That's understandable, considering the kind of histories they have and the leagues they play in. But in Chicago, there's more than enough room for teams from other leagues and the occasional major event. No, the money isn't as great and the headlines aren't as big, but these franchises don't get lost in the shuffle.

The Fire are the most popular of these teams, but they're hardly alone. Others include the Chicago Sky of the Women's National Basketball Association, the Chicago Wolves of the American Hockey League, the Chicago Red Stars of the National Women's Soccer

League, and the most recent addition, the Windy City Bulls of the G League. These teams have their fan bases and history.

The Wolves entered the old International Hockey League in 1994, and it was at the perfect time. The NHL was in the middle of a costly lockout, and the Blackhawks were a couple of years away from their nosedive. The Wolves capitalized by becoming a winner on the ice—claiming the first of four league titles in 1998—and shrewdly marketing themselves as the affordable, family-friendly, and winning alternative to the Blackhawks. And though the Blackhawks have returned to the top of the Chicago sports scene, the Wolves have carved out a successful and long-lasting niche playing in the second-tier American Hockey League.

▲ After a successful stint in England's Premier League, Arlington Heights native Brian McBride returned in 2008 to end his career with the Fire.

Founded in 2006, the Sky have had their moments. In 2013, the team picked a guard/forward from the University of Delaware named Elena Delle Donne, who briefly transformed the underachieving franchise. Along with Olympic gold medalist and defensive superstar Sylvia Fowles, the Sky made their first playoff appearance in 2013 and reached the WNBA Finals in 2014. Although both players were gone by 2017, a planned 2018 move to 10,387-seat Wintrust Arena just south of downtown is intended to put the Sky more thoroughly in the spotlight after their time in suburban Rosemont.

"On behalf of basketball fans across the city, we want to welcome the Chicago Sky to their new home right here in Chicago," Mayor Rahm Emanuel said in a statement when the move was announced.

FIVE STARS FROM
BEYOND THE FIVE

Cuauhtemoc Blanco (Fire, 2007–2009)

Blanco stayed for only three years, but he came to define an era of Fire soccer. A legendary figure in Mexico, he brought the team hordes of new Mexican fans and energized the city for its soccer team. As one of the league's first "designated players," meaning his salary wasn't limited by the cap, Blanco made MLS viable in Mexico and helped add to its worldwide reputation. What David Beckham was for MLS, Blanco was for the Fire.

Elena Delle Donne (Sky, 2013–2016)

Delle Donne's exit from Chicago after the 2016 season wasn't graceful, as she forced a trade to the Washington Mystics. Before that, she was the face of the Sky and one of the greatest players in the world. The unanimous 2013 Rookie of the Year and winner of the 2015 MVP Award, Delle Donne also served as an activist for many causes, including Lyme disease and the Special Olympics.

Back in the suburbs, Toyota Park has hosted some of the region's lesser-known teams, including the Chicago Bliss lingerie football team and Major League Lacrosse's Chicago Machine. The Fire's most prominent roommate, though, is the Red Stars. Having survived multiple women's pro soccer leagues, the team found stability with the 2013 founding of the NWSL. With one of the city's most underrated logos, the team has featured several top players, including US stars Lori Chalupny, Julie Ertz (née Johnston), and Christen Press.

Sylvia Fowles (Sky, 2008–2014)

Delle Donne was great with the Sky, but she wouldn't have won anything there if not for Fowles. A dominant center, Fowles won two defensive player of the year awards in Chicago and also took home two Olympic gold medals. Unfortunately for the Sky, Fowles forced a trade to Minnesota after the 2014 WNBA Finals loss to Phoenix, short-circuiting what could have been one of the league's best teams.

Steve Maltais (Wolves, 1994–2005)

If there's one player responsible for the Wolves establishing themselves in Chicago, it's Maltais. He holds the team record in goals (454), assists (497), and points (951) and was part of three league-championship teams. Maltais appeared in 120 NHL games over six seasons, but he's best remembered for his role in building one of minor league hockey's strongest organizations.

Piotr "Peter" Nowak (Fire, 1998–2002)

If you're the captain of a team that won a double (MLS Cup and US Open Cup) in its first year, you're on this list. Nowak, however, did more than just captain the 1998 Fire. A veteran of multiple German leagues, Nowak was the 1998 MLS Cup MVP and gave his new team instant credibility with his experience and toughness bred in some of Europe's best competitions. He also was a hit with the city's Polish soccer fans and helped draw them to the fledgling team. In fact, to this day the Fire are linked with any prominent Polish player, whether or not there's any actual interest.

The City of Big Events

Centrally located. Big stadiums. Rabid fans. Corporate money.

It figures that Chicago would be a hub for more than just the major professional and college teams. The city has become a destination for big international sporting events, including some of the most famous events in the world.

Perhaps the jewel of the local calendar is the Chicago Marathon, which regularly draws some of the world's top marathoners and was featured in the 2007 cult-favorite running documentary *Spirit of the Marathon*. But turn the sports calendar and you'll see the city has also hosted triathlon world championships, famous boxing matches, and major golf tournaments. It has hosted auto racing, horse racing, and even boat racing. In fact, just about any big event looking for an audience on US soil at least considers Chicago, which is how the city became an enthusiastic home to . . . rugby. Yes, rugby.

In 2014, the iconic New Zealand All Blacks faced the United States in a friendly match at Soldier Field. But the event was much more than just a friendly. The game was a coming-out party for rugby and its efforts to become America's next sport. The match was broadcast on national television, and more than 61,000 fans jammed into Soldier Field to watch one of world sports' most famous teams in this most unusual of venues. The All Blacks performed their Haka and then rolled past an overmatched US team, winning 74–6. In some ways, though, the result didn't matter; it was just a cool spectacle.

If rugby is America's next sport, then it's taking the label away from soccer. Chicago played a major role in that sport's rise to the mainstream in the United States, too, starting with the 1994 World Cup. The landmark event held its opening ceremony in Chicago. President Bill Clinton visited, and Oprah Winfrey emceed, although the event might be best remembered for Diana Ross shanking a penalty kick as part of her live performance.

As for the soccer itself, Soldier Field hosted four matches in group play and another in the knockout phase. Future Fire star Hristo Stoichkov scored two of his six total goals in Chicago as his upstart Bulgaria team marched on to a surprise fourth-place finish. Germany and Belgium played a round of 16 game at Soldier Field, and legends of the game including Germany's Jurgen Klinsmann and Lothar Matthäus and Spain's Luis Enrique were among those who graced the pitch in Chicago.

Five years later, Soldier Field played host to four group-stage matches during the 1999 Women's World Cup, including one for the eventual champion United States. And although that game looked like a walk in the park—it ended in a 7–1 win over Nigeria— Nigeria scored first and threw a scare into the US team and the 65,000 fans in attendance, then an absurd number for women's soccer.

Soldier Field has continued to host numerous other major soccer events, ranging from the Copa America Centenario to the Gold Cup to friendlies featuring teams such as Manchester United, Real Madrid, and Paris Saint-Germain.

Before soccer registered to most Americans, Chicago was the scene for some of boxing's most memorable moments. Sugar Ray Robinson brutally beat Jake LaMotta in a 1951 fight at Chicago Stadium, Sonny Liston knocked out Floyd Patterson in 1962 at Comiskey Park, and Joe Louis beat "Cinderella Man" James Braddock with an eighth-round knockout in 1937 at Comiskey Park.

But the most famous—or infamous—bout took place at Soldier Field on September 22, 1927. Former champion Jack Dempsey looked to regain his heavyweight title from Gene Tunney and struggled until the seventh round, when he hit Tunney's jaw. For whatever reason, Dempsey didn't retreat to a neutral corner for five seconds, delaying the count. Tunney got up at the nine-count by referee Dave Barry, meaning he had been down for almost 15 seconds, and won on a unanimous decision, ending Dempsey's career.

Over the years, golf has found a home in the Chicago area. In 1899, the Western Open was staged for the first time, and from 1962 to 2006, it was played every year in the area. Winners included Tiger Woods, Tom Watson, Jack Nicklaus, and Arnold Palmer. The tournament was renamed the BMW Championship in 2007 and now is held every other year in Chicagoland. Other major tournaments have also found a home in the Windy City. The Chicago area has held six PGA Championships, and the US Open has come to Chicago 13 times, most recently in 2003. Perhaps most memorable, though, was the 2012 Ryder Cup at Medinah. Fans saw the United States blow a 10–6 lead on the final day to lose the Cup 14 ½–13 ½.

Even auto racing has settled into the area. Chicagoland Speedway in Joliet hosts an annual NASCAR race, and from 1999 to 2002, Chicago Motor Speedway, formerly Sportsman's Park horse racing course, welcomed open-wheel racing.

When it comes to big-time events, few cities anywhere can compare.

FORE Bubba Watson of the US team hits his tee shot on the first hole at the 2012 Ryder Cup in Medinah.

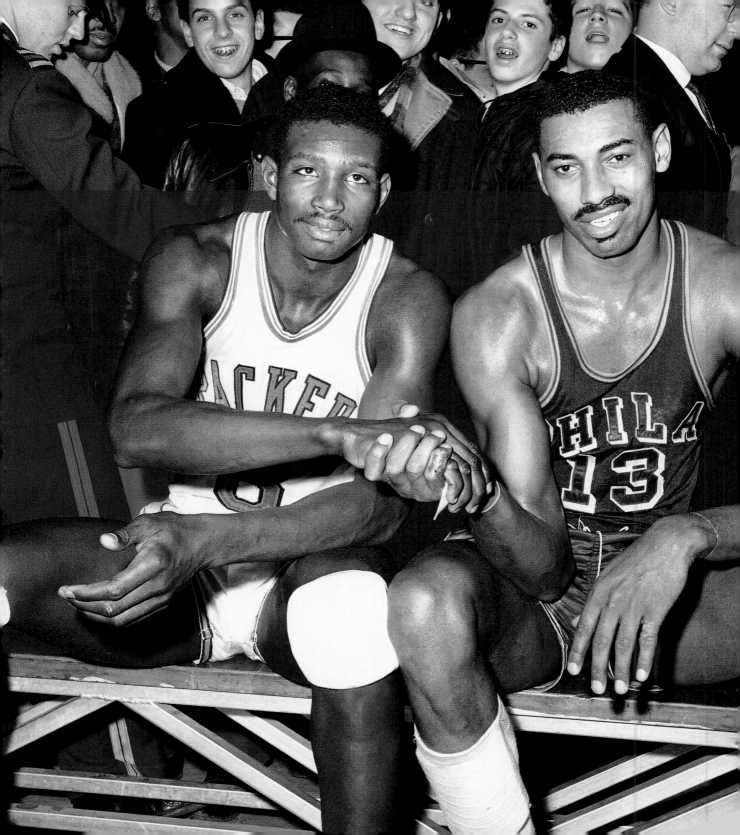

CHAPTER 9

GONE, NOT FORGOTTEN

Not even a great sports town like Chicago has a perfect record. Some teams have simply not made it. And when it comes to hoops, Chicago had a well-earned reputation as the "graveyard of professional basketball." The Chicago American Gears of the National Basketball League folded in 1947 despite having a young center named George Mikan. The Chicago Stags followed and had some success but folded in 1950, leaving the city without a major basketball team for 11 years. Up next were the unfortunately named Packers, who changed their name after a year to Zephyrs but then moved to Baltimore and are now the Washington Wizards.

Whether it was because of poor marketing, bad ownership, mediocre arenas, or the popularity of the other sports teams, Chicago and pro basketball just didn't work until the Bulls came around in 1966.

◀ Even the presence of future Hall of Famer Walt Bellamy, shown here as a rookie with Wilt Chamberlain, couldn't save the ill-conceived Chicago Packers.

As the NHL raced to expand its footprint in the late 1960s and early 1970s, the World Hockey Association arrived in 1972 to try to grab some of that market share. Among the 12 teams in the WHA's inaugural 1972–73 season was a Chicago entrant, the Cougars. Playing home games at the International Amphitheatre, the Cougars survived three seasons in the WHA and even made the 1974 league final, but ultimately the team—and the league—was unable to compete with the NHL and folded.

Pro soccer made a run of it in the 1970s, too, with the North American Soccer League in its Pelé-inspired heyday. The Sting represented Chicago in the boom-or-bust NASL from 1975 to 1984, winning two league titles and occasionally drawing large crowds to Wrigley Field and Comiskey Park before ending their existence as an indoor team in 1988. The Sting won the final NASL outdoor title in 1984 and still have a crew of die-hard fans that would like to see the franchise return in one form or another.

Minor league baseball teams have come and gone, and from 1914 to 1915 it can be argued Chicago had three big-league teams when the Whales played in the Federal League. Though the Whales won the 1915 Federal League pennant with players such as Mordecai Brown and Joe Tinker, their greatest legacy is the little diamond they left behind at Clark and Addison, now known as Wrigley Field.

And for one reason or another, Chicago has also had its share of football teams. Some, like the Chicago Fire and Chicago Winds of the short-lived World Football League, the Chicago Rockets of the All-America Football Conference, or the Chicago Blitz of the doomed United States Football League, had little impact on the city. The less said about the XFL the better, but Chicago's Enforcers were a relatively competent team coached by Ron Meyer and made the league semifinals in their lone year of existence.

The indoor game has also had spurts of success. The Bruisers were the city's first arena team and lasted three seasons before disbanding in 1989. The Rush followed in 2001, won an Arena Bowl in 2006, and routinely drew capacity crowds to Allstate Arena before the bottom fell out and the team folded in 2013.

Of course, the team that left the greatest mark was the Chicago Cardinals. Founded as the Morgan Athletic Club, the Cardinals were in Chicago before the Bears and can be considered the oldest surviving pro football team in the United States. At various times they played their home games at Comiskey Park, Wrigley Field, and

▲ Despite their best efforts, the Chicago Cougars couldn't make it work in the WHA.

Soldier Field, and they had great players such as Charley Trippi, Ollie Matson, and Dick "Night Train" Lane. Still, the team was in dire straits before moving to St. Louis in 1960.

The city even hosted the annual preseason College All-Star Game from 1934 to 1976, pitting a team of the previous season's best college football players against the reigning NFL or Super Bowl champions. Increasingly a nuisance for everybody involved, the game was discontinued after the 1976 edition that was canceled in the third quarter because of heavy rain and the fans that stormed the field to slide on the soaked turf.

Could the Cardinals Have Made It?

For all the teams Chicago has lost, the one that hurts the most is the NFL Cardinals, leaving behind a simple question: What if they had stayed?

A perennial contender in the late 1940s that won the 1947 NFL championship and returned to the title game the next year, the Cardinals' fall in the 1950s was quick and steep. Simply put, the Chicago Cardinals of the 1950s were not a successful organization.

Always struggling for attention in the shadow of the burgeoning Bears behemoth, the Cardinals' swan dive into the NFL's depths was not well timed. The team had just one winning season in the 1950s and employed a parade of coaches. Despite the presence of stars including Ollie Matson and Dick "Night Train" Lane, coaches such as Curly Lambeau, Phil Handler, Joe Kuharich, Joe Stydahar, Ray Richards, and Pop Ivy failed to turn around the franchise. After a surprising 7–5 season in 1956, the bottom fell out. The 1957 team won three games, the 1958 team went 2–9–1, and the 1959 group was 2–10.

By this point, the future of the team was clearly in jeopardy. Attendance at Comiskey Park was plummeting. The 1957 season ended with a 27–2 loss to the Steelers in front of 10,084 at Comiskey Park. In 1958, the team played three home games in front of crowds of fewer than 20,000.

Understandably, vultures were circling to buy the broke and broken franchise and move it to another market. Walter Wolfner owned the team and took offers from

Bud Adams and Lamar Hunt, among others, to purchase the franchise, but nothing came of those talks. Despite wanting to fight George Halas and the Bears for Chicago, Wolfner eventually wanted to move the team but couldn't because the NFL was demanding sky-high relocation fees. Halas, for his part, was believed to be trying to force the Cardinals out of Chicago.

One example of Halas's interference was the Cards' efforts to move to Dyche Stadium on the Northwestern campus. Wolfner claimed he had a deal with the school, but Halas came up with a 28-year-old agreement that said the Cardinals couldn't play on the North Side and the Bears couldn't play on the south.

"That agreement wasn't worth the paper it was written on," Wolfner said in 1960, "but (commissioner Bert) Bell gave it the force of law by stepping in and ruling that it was valid. If we had moved to Dyche Stadium, we wouldn't be leaving Chicago now."

In 1959, the Cardinals' future was clearly not in Chicago, but it was unclear where the team was headed. It moved into cavernous Soldier Field and played a pair of home games at Metropolitan Stadium in suburban Minneapolis. Meanwhile, Adams and Hunt were unable to buy an NFL team and instead formed the American Football League.

The new league was set to begin in 1960. So, the NFL, wanting to block the upstarts from claiming St. Louis, allowed the Cardinals to move to the Gateway City, ending their stay in Chicago.

At the time, the move looked like a smart one. Despite sharing a name with the baseball team, the Cardinals finally had a football city of their own. By 1966, Big Red played at modern Busch Stadium and finally had a contemporary home.

▲ Fans can only wonder what Chicago's sports scene would be like today had the Cardinals found a way to make it work.

That said, football isn't the first love of St. Louis, and the football Cardinals were never fully embraced there before leaving in 1988. Who knows, maybe things could have worked out in Chicago if they had stayed. When the Cardinals left, pro football was just beginning its boom. New York supported two football teams (Giants and Titans), while Chicago was already supporting two teams in baseball.

There's no reason the Cardinals couldn't have survived in Chicago if they had found a way to be better on the field. Unlike the Bears, who lingered in a baseball stadium for 11 more years, the Cardinals were looking to move into a bigger stadium more suitable for football. And like the White Sox, they could have truly become the South Side's team, building a rivalry with the Bears that's similar to the one shared by the Cubs and White Sox.

Alas, it never happened. The Cardinals moved in 1960, and the Bears own Chicago football. It might have been fun to see the Cardinals stay. Unfortunately, we'll never know how it would have worked.

THE GREATEST OF
THE GHOSTS

Their teams are gone, but their impacts are still felt to this day. Here are the five greatest players or coaches from teams that no longer call Chicago home.

Walt Bellamy (Packers/Zephyrs: 1961–1963)

Bellamy was the No. 1 overall pick in the 1961 draft and lived up to the billing. A 6'11" center, he averaged 31.6 points and 19 rebounds per game as a rookie and followed that up by averaging 27.9 points and 16.4 boards for the franchise now known as the Zephyrs. Bellamy was dealt to the Knicks in 1965 and inducted into the Hall of Fame in 1993.

Ollie Matson (Cardinals: 1952–1958)

A running back and wide receiver, Matson was an Olympic sprinter and won Olympic medals in the 400-meter run and 4x400 relay in 1952. He used that speed in Chicago. Playing on increasingly poor Cardinals teams, Matson was a six-time All-Pro in Chicago before getting dealt to the Rams for nine players in 1959.

Willy Roy (Sting: 1975, 1977–1986)

Roy came to the Sting as a player in 1975 and was named the head coach in 1979 after spending time as an assistant. Roy spearheaded the influx of German players on the team, and it paid off, taking the Sting to NASL titles in 1981 and 1984, the latter being the last outdoor title in league history.

Charley Trippi (Cardinals: 1947–1955)

Trippi was a versatile halfback and part of the "Million Dollar Backfield" that led the Cardinals to the 1947 NFL title and an appearance in the 1948 championship game. A Hall of Famer, Trippi is part of the 1940s all-decade team. That 1947 title was the last in Cardinals history.

Max Zaslofsky (Stags: 1946–1950)

Zaslofsky was one of pro basketball's first great scorers. He led the Basketball Association of America (the predecessor to the NBA) in total scoring in 1947–48 and was a four-time member of the league's first team. In 1956, he ended his career as the third-leading scorer in NBA history.

CHAPTER 10
CHICAGO'S VERY OWN

Let's set the scene.

It's a crisp fall day in early October. The leaves are starting to change, and the shadows are getting a little longer. Chicago is at its most beautiful as the sun rises. And the city unites to watch runners from all over the world compete in one of its greatest annual spectacles.

It's the Chicago Marathon, an event that showcases the gorgeous metropolis to the world. The race traces its roots back to 1905, but it has thrived particularly since the modern era began in 1977. Today it's one of the biggest and most prestigious marathons in the world, with 44,508 crossing the finish line in 2017. Along the course you'll see all sorts of neighborhoods and architecture, and Chicagoans cheering on the competitors.

There is nothing more Chicago than this event. But it's just one of many sporting events that is uniquely Chicago.

◀ US Olympian Galen Rupp crosses the finish line first at the 2017 Chicago Marathon.

The Miracle Million

The 1985 Arlington Million shouldn't have been held at Arlington Park. No way, no how. It was impossible.

On July 31, 1985, a small fire started in the old grandstand, which had stood since 1927. The fire became bigger and bigger, and before it was put out the blaze had claimed the entire grandstand and clubhouse. Certainly, the annual Arlington Million, scheduled for August 25, would be canceled or moved to another facility.

Nope. Not gonna happen. The race would go on as scheduled.

"I had made a commitment to horse owners from all around the world, some of whom had already shipped their horses over," track owner Richard Duchossois said. "Some people said it would be impossible, but I said: 'I'm the owner, and we're going to run the Million race. Period.'"

The fire destroyed pretty much everything at Arlington—except for the turf track. That gave Arlington a chance to host the race, but work had to be done.

"I remember that on August 4, Mr. Duchossois gathered us all together and said, 'We're going to run the Arlington Million right here in 21 days.' None of us thought it was possible," said Bill Thayer, Arlington's executive vice president. "The only guy who knew it was possible was Dick Duchossois. Thank God for that."

A MILLION DOLLARS Since the first running in 1981, the Arlington Million thoroughbred turf race has been a summer tradition in the northwest suburbs.

It was possible, but it happened because of hard work. Crews worked 10 hours at a time to build temporary stands and facilities. Tents and temporary bleachers went up in the blink of an eye.

More than 35,000 fans crammed into the facility on race day to watch the Million. Teleprompter was the winning horse, but in truth everybody from Arlington and the Chicago racing community were the winners.

In a fitting postscript, Arlington Park became the first track to win an Eclipse Award, a top honor in the sport. The plaque says: "In recognition of the indomitable spirit of the officers and staff for a 'Miracle.' Well Done."

Chicago's Hoop Dreams

Chicago's basketball scene isn't just the Bulls or DePaul.

There's so much more to it, and some of the most intense games can be found in high school gyms across the city. Perhaps no city has a better high school basketball scene. Not only are the games competitive, but the teams and players are among the best in the nation.

The Chicago Public League is a cradle for too much talent to list here. Derrick Rose, Jabari Parker, Kevin Garnett, Ronnie Fields, and Jahlil Okafor are just five of the all-time greatest who graced city courts and became Chicago legends. Before a reorganization, the Public League tournament crowned the city champion—and the only Chicago team to travel downstate to the Elite Eight.

"Back then King and Simeon, and Marshall or Collins or Westinghouse . . . we would have been downstate every year," former King coach Landon "Sonny" Cox told the *Chicago Tribune* in 2007, five years after the format was changed to allow multiple Public League teams to go downstate.

Even with the new format, the passion is still strong. It's just as strong through the Chicago Catholic League, too, and all of the public and private suburban schools. The talent doesn't just stop at the city limits. The 'burbs have sent their share of talent to major colleges and the NBA. Isiah Thomas played at St. Joseph, Candace Parker competed at Naperville Central, and Doc Rivers starred at Proviso East.

"Proviso East is what it is," Rivers said in 2012. "You know what it is. It's a heck of a school. For basketball, I don't know if there's any place better in the country, not only in the state, as far as the history of it."

If you're looking to learn about the Chicago hoops scene (and Chicago in general), there's no better movie than the 1994 classic *Hoop Dreams*. The movie follows prep prospects William Gates and Arthur Agee from middle school all the way to college. It dives deeply into their lives and pulls no punches about the seedier aspects of city living and trying to make it in basketball. But it also is an inspiring look at two young men and their love of the game. And a city's love of the game.

▲ Before turning the NBA upside down as the first high school draft pick in two decades, Kevin Garnett was the 1995 Mr. Basketball while leading Farragut Academy to its first Public League championship.

"Many filmgoers are reluctant to see documentaries, for reasons I've never understood; the good ones are frequently more absorbing and entertaining than fiction. *Hoop Dreams*, however, is not only a documentary. It is also poetry and prose, muckraking and exposé, journalism and polemic," film critic Roger Ebert wrote in the *Chicago Sun-Times*. "It is one of the great moviegoing experiences of my lifetime."

The East-West All-Star Game and the Negro Leagues

Every year at Guaranteed Rate Field, the White Sox host the Double Duty Classic. Named for Chicago American Giants star Ted "Double Duty" Radcliffe, the game is a showdown between the best inner-city baseball players in the country and helps teach youth about the Negro Leagues and what they meant to baseball and much of America.

"Each year, we have seen young men participate in the event, learn and grow from the experience here—not only on the field, but in their careers away from the field and at home," White Sox vice president of community relations Christine O'Reilly said. "It is so important to us that we continue to share the incredible legacy of the Negro Leagues with the next generation so that we never take for granted the sacrifice and dedication of those men who played in order to give others a chance to play."

It's also fitting that the White Sox have taken the lead in this initiative. During their heyday, the Negro Leagues had a massive and important presence in Chicago. One team stood above the rest.

Frank Leland and W.S. Peters founded the Chicago Union Giants in 1887, and the team was renamed the Leland Giants in 1905. In 1910, Andrew "Rube" Foster took control

SHOWTIME Negro Leagues icon Josh Gibson slides into home during the East-West All-Star Game in 1944 at Comiskey Park.

of the franchise and renamed it the Chicago American Giants one year later. Foster went on to form the Negro National League, one of two preeminent all-black major leagues, with his team being a charter member. Today, American Giants gear is still prevalent around the city, and the White Sox have played throwback games wearing their uniforms.

The Negro Leagues, of course, meant more than just baseball. They were a pillar of the black community and a source of pride. Despite battling segregation and hatred, players took their game across the country to try to eke out a living. Games were intense and hard but as good and entertaining as anything you'd see on any diamond anywhere.

To have such an impact, the Negro Leagues needed strong leaders, and few were as important as Foster.

"From about 1911 until 1926, he stood astride Negro baseball in the Midwest with unchallenged power, a friend of Major League leaders, and the best-known black man in Chicago. Rube Foster was an unfettered genius who combined generosity and sternness, the superb skills of a dedicated athlete, and an unbounded belief in the future of the black baseball player," Robert Peterson wrote in *Only the Ball Was White*. "His life was baseball. Had he chose otherwise, baseball would have been the poorer."

Baseball was certainly richer because of Foster, and Chicago was certainly a better baseball town because of the Negro Leagues. Comiskey Park annually hosted the best black players in the game at the East-West All-Star Game. Founded in 1933, the same year as the MLB version, the Negro League legends converged on Comiskey to play intense games. Stars included Satchel Paige, Martin Dihigo, Josh Gibson, and Jackie Robinson.

"You got a chance to play and throw against the very best," Newark Eagles pitcher Leon Day said. "It always gave you a little extra, a little something pumping through your blood."

That legacy still pumps through the blood of Chicago baseball. Everybody is better for it.

> "You got a chance to play and throw against the very best. It always gave you a little extra, a little something pumping through your blood."
>
> - Leon **DAY**
> PITCHER, NEWARK EAGLES

TRUE GIANT As owner-manager of the Chicago American Giants, Rube Foster was instrumental in creating the Negro National League in 1920.

12 LOCAL ATHLETES WHO
LEFT AND THRIVED

Jesus Chavez

Chavez was born in Mexico but raised in Chicago. During a boxing career that spanned from 1994 to 2010, he was a world champion at two weight classes. He went 44–8 with 30 knockouts, though his path to stardom was interrupted when at age 16 he was convicted of being an accessory to armed robbery and deported.

"I learned the majority of my basic boxing skills in Chicago," he said.

Otto Graham

Graham was born in Waukegan and didn't stray far for college, going to Northwestern. Graham originally played basketball at NU and didn't join the football team until his sophomore year. He signed with the All-America Football Conference's Cleveland Browns in 1946 and established himself as one of pro football's most successful quarterbacks before retiring in 1955. He won four AAFC titles and three NFL crowns, and he took home three NFL MVP Awards in his Hall of Fame career.

"Otto Graham was the greatest player in the game's history," Browns coach Paul Brown said in his autobiography.

Mike Krzyzewski

Coach K grew up on the Near North Side and graduated from West Point in 1969. He played basketball there under Bob Knight and eventually became a coach, taking over at Army in 1975 and Duke in 1980. At Duke, Coach K turned a sleeping giant into the game's most powerful program. In 2017, he won his 1,000th game at Duke, and he's the first men's coach overall to win 1,000 Division I games. He has five national titles and three Olympic gold medals and is in the conversation for greatest basketball coach of all time.

Marv Levy

Levy graduated from South Shore High School in 1943 and embarked on a long football career. As a head coach, he led the Montreal Alouettes to Grey Cup wins in 1974 and 1977, he coached the Kansas City Chiefs from 1978 to 1982, and he led the United States Football League's Chicago Blitz in 1984. But his greatest success came in Buffalo. From 1986 to 1997, he led the Bills to prominence, taking them to four straight Super Bowls while coaching Jim Kelly, Bruce Smith, Thurman Thomas, and one of the NFL's most talented teams.

"It is said that leadership is that unique quality which enables special people to stand up and pull the rest of us over the horizon," said Bill Polian when he presented Levy at his 2001 Hall of Fame ceremony. "By that or any other definition, Marv Levy is one of the greatest leaders this game has ever known."

Brian McBride

An Arlington Heights native, McBride was with the Fire from 2008 to 2010, but by then his legacy had been well established. A striker, he was the first draft pick in MLS history, taken by Columbus in 1996, and spent eight years with the Crew. From there he went to England, where he proved that American outfield players could thrive in the Premier League. In five seasons with Fulham, from 2004 to 2008, McBride became one of the team's most consistent scorers and was eventually named captain. His play for the Cottagers helped open up the Premier League for a host of other Americans. And yet that might not even be his greatest legacy. Over a 12-year career with the US men's national team, McBride scored 30 goals in 95 appearances, including playing key roles on the 1998, 2002, and 2006 World Cup teams.

George Mikan

Mikan was the first basketball superstar, and he got his start in suburban Joliet. From there he went to DePaul, where he teamed with coach Ray Meyer to lead the Blue Demons to the 1945 National Invitation Tournament title. After college, Mikan spent a season with the Chicago American Gears, who folded in 1947. The Minneapolis Lakers then acquired him, and the rest was history. A center, he won five NBA titles with Minneapolis and dominated basketball as few ever had. The lane was widened because of him, and in response to teams stalling against the Lakers, the league instituted the 24-second shot clock.

"He was the greatest impact player of that era," Bob Cousy said. "He was a big man who could do so many things on the court. He literally transcended the sport, and he created such visibility. In the 1940s and '50s, he was the marquee player. He lifted us out of the doldrums and made the league respectable."

▶ George Mikan

12 LOCAL ATHLETES WHO
LEFT AND THRIVED

Ray Nitschke

Nitschke would have been the perfect Bear. But the tough, mean, ferocious linebacker, who played at Proviso East and the University of Illinois, didn't end up in Chicago. He ended up in Green Bay, becoming the leader of the Lombardi-era defense and winning five NFL titles and the first two Super Bowls.

"He was the man. He was a guy who played with a lot of great tenacity. Every time you saw him, you knew he was ready to play," Packers teammate Willie Wood said. "He had that ability to make people like him, and for that I would never forget him."

Candace Parker

The Naperville-raised Parker might not be the greatest women's basketball player of all time, but she's in the conversation. Parker became the first woman to dunk twice in an NCAA Tournament game and won two national titles at Tennessee. A two-time Olympic gold medalist, Parker was the No. 1 overall pick in the 2008 WNBA draft and led the Los Angeles Sparks to the 2016 WNBA title after a long wait for her first ring.

"This is her life, her legacy; this is what you dream of," Cynthia Cooper said. "This is why she works hard every day; this is why you sacrifice for these moments. I know Candace Parker is feeling like it's all worth it."

Kirby Puckett

Puckett was raised in a housing project on the South Side and fought through his tough upbringing and unimpressive physique to become one of the greatest Minnesota Twins ever. He won two World Series titles and forever will be remembered for what he did in the 1991 World Series. In Game 6, his leaping catch at the wall robbed Ron Gant of extra bases, and he ended the game with a walk-off homer off Charlie Leibrandt in the 11th inning to cap one of the greatest single performances in World Series history.

"We were in a bad way; we needed someone to step forward in a major way," teammate Gene Larkin said. "He told us to jump on his back. Not many guys can talk the talk and walk the walk, but Kirby always could. After he spoke to us, we just knew that Kirby was going to do something special. We've seen him do that many times. That time it was on the biggest stage."

Barney Ross

Ross, one of the world's best boxers, was active from 1929 to 1938. He was a champion lightweight, junior welterweight, and welterweight. Ross also fought in another, more important battle: World War II, enlisting in the Marines in 1942.

Isiah Thomas

The way Isiah Thomas and the Pistons beat the Bulls in the late 1980s and 1990 might have hurt a bit more because of where Thomas started. Raised on the West Side, Thomas went to state powerhouse St. Joseph High School in Westchester and went on to lead the University of Indiana to a national championship. Thomas then keyed the Pistons' rise and was the leader of the Bad Boys team that won two titles and was loathed by all Bulls fans.

"Simply put, Isiah Thomas was the difference maker and the key to the franchise's success," said former Pistons president and CEO Tom Wilson.

Dwyane Wade

The less said about Wade's Bulls career the better, but nobody can doubt the impact the Richards High School graduate has had on the NBA. He led Marquette University to the 2003 Final Four and was taken fifth overall by the Heat in the 2003 draft. Wade and Shaquille O'Neal combined to power Miami to the 2006 title, and Wade became a global icon. He then helped create Miami's Big Three, wooing LeBron James and Chris Bosh to the Heat, where they combined to win two titles and four conference crowns.

"I came here ready to play basketball, and look what that's done with me," Wade said. "I came here to play basketball, work my butt off, and get to it. And I've gotten to it for 13 years. It's not all been great. It's been some amazing years, some in-here years, and for our team, some down-here years. But it's been a special journey. But as I sit here and look back today, I wouldn't do nothing different."

▶ Ray Nitschke

CHICAGO'S MOUNT RUSHMORE

Of all the sports figures in Chicago's history, four stand out. One was a fun-loving personality who always kept things positive, even as losses and frustration piled up around him. Another built the foundation of an iconic team and a powerful league that's growing to this day. Then there's simply the greatest athlete in history, the one who redefined a city in ways athletes usually don't. Finally, one endeared himself to Chicagoans with his work ethic and refusal to back down from any challenge.

These are the four who built Chicago sports, defined its character, defined its personality, and lifted it to its greatest heights. In short, you can't write a detailed history of Chicago sports without them.

◄ Chicago has no shortage of legendary sports figures, but Ernie Banks, George Halas, Michael Jordan, and Walter Payton stand above the rest.

Ernie *BANKS*

SHORTSTOP AND FIRST BASEMAN - CHICAGO CUBS (1953—1971)

Ernie Banks never won a World Series. He never played in a playoff game, never finished first, and his best seasons came before the Cubs were a contender. The best team he ever played on blew a nine-game lead in August and finished eight games out of first place.

But there's more to Banks's legacy than his 512 home runs, his two National League MVP Awards, and his sparkling play. The team's first black player, Banks personified the faith and hope that Cubs fans all share, that this year would be the year. And every day was a gift, made even better if the Cubs were playing two.

"It was a very bad day in Chicago," Banks said, explaining his famous slogan. "I came into the locker room, and I was feeling great. And I said to all my teammates, 'It's a beautiful day—let's play two!' That was a time in my life that I was really excited about going to Wrigley Field."

That's what Banks really was.

He made people happy, made people smile, and always showed people the power of positivity. That would be impressive for anybody, but even more so considering his bumpy path to the majors and the lack of team success he experienced when he got there.

"I guess my critics say, 'He must be crazy. Nothing can be that beautiful,' " Banks said. "But when you think that there are so many people around the world who have nothing, you realize how lucky you are to be making a living in the big leagues. There's an unbelievable, indescribable love for baseball in Wrigley Field."

And Banks was a truly great ballplayer.

He was the first true power-hitting shortstop, cranking out at least 40 homers for four straight seasons (1957–1960). He played a Cubs-record 2,528 games and was the first player to have his number retired by the team. Banks was also durable, playing in at least 150 games 12 times.

"He was a pleasure to be around," Joe Amalfitano said. "It's a shame he never went to the playoffs, but he was that rare person who was talented, was full of energy, and gave you the feeling you could win."

Banks joined the Cubs in 1953, but his pro career actually began in 1950 when, as a 19-year-old, he signed with the Kansas City Monarchs, one of the most prominent Negro Leagues teams. Playing under the iconic Buck O'Neill, Banks hit .255 in 1950 before missing two seasons to serve in the US Army. When he returned in 1953 a more mature athlete, he was ready to handle top-tier pitching and batted .347.

"Playing for the Kansas City Monarchs was like my school, my learning, my world," Banks said. "It was my whole life."

Banks's life made him a Chicago icon during his playing career and after it. He was a beloved figure who routinely made appearances around Wrigley Field. Fans clamored to be in his presence, and not just because of what kind of player he was, but because of the way he related to fans.

When the Cubs finally won the World Series in 2016, Banks had been gone for almost two years. While former teammates Billy Williams and Ferguson Jenkins basked in the glow of the Cubs finally winning it all, there was something missing. Everybody who watched the triumph wondered just how Ernie Banks would've reacted.

He would've been happy and proud of what his team had done. But more than that, he deserved to have seen what happened, and to get the championship ring he richly deserved.

George *HALAS*

END, COACH, OWNER - CHICAGO BEARS (1920–1983)

Forget for a moment about the Bears. What would American sports look like if not for Halas? He didn't just help create the NFL, but by extension he created what would become the country's behemoth sports league and one of the most powerful and influential cartels in the country. No sport has ingrained itself into American culture like pro football, dominating Sundays—one-seventh of the week—for some 20 weeks every fall and winter.

That started with Halas.

As for the Bears, Halas was their founder and inspiration. For parts of seven decades, Halas was the Bears, and the Bears were a reflection of his personality. They played the game the way he wanted: with toughness and feistiness that would brutalize opponents.

"The thing that really annoyed me, as a competitor, when you went to Wrigley Field, was that Halas actually would sell seats on our bench to patrons of the Bears," Rams linebacker Don Paul said. "The rope would be right behind you, and the fans would be standing directly behind you, with the obscenities in your ear while you're trying to hear what's going on to play a football game."

"He was a tyrant up and down the sidelines," defensive end Ed Sprinkle said.

Tyrant, yes. Try to gain an advantage here and there, sure. Careful with money and salaries? Many Bears players would agree. But Halas was a visionary and a damn good football player and coach, too. On the field, Halas played a season with the semi-professional Hammond All Stars and then more than a decade with the Staleys and Bears. He was an end on offense and defense and even was named to the NFL's All-Pro team for the 1920s.

Before that, he was part of the Great Lakes Naval Training Station team that beat the Mare Island Marines 17–0 in the 1919 Rose Bowl.

"That game was my greatest thrill as a player," Halas said. "I scored a touchdown on a pass from Paddy Driscoll, and I intercepted a pass and ran 79 yards before being caught from behind on the 1. My more artistic satisfaction as a player was playing against Jim Thorpe. He could cut you down with his legs, and he could throw a defensive body block at top speed that still echoes."

As a coach, Halas won championships in four decades and retired as the winningest coach in NFL history, with 318 victories. As an executive, his last major moves included keeping Buddy Ryan as the defensive coordinator and hiring Mike Ditka as head coach, both of whom were integral in the 1985 Bears winning Super Bowl XX.

There was a possibility football would have needed to thrive without Halas. Before his association with the Bears, Halas was expected to be a big part of the New York Yankees, even playing in 13 games during the 1919 season.

"It is unusual for a college player to jump into the big leagues and become a regular the first season, but this is just the thing that Halas threatens to do," the *New York Times* wrote in 1919. "He is swift afoot and is a heady and proficient base runner. He covers a lot of ground in the outfield, and best of all he is a world of enthusiasm for the game."

Lingering injuries did him in. But what if he hadn't failed in baseball? Would he eventually have become a star baseball player and part of the Yankees' dynasty, leaving football to grow with somebody else's vision?

What would American sports be without Halas? What would the city of Chicago look like without Halas? The best question is, what would American culture have been like without Halas? Because of him, a day of a week is defined by a sport. Halas's sport.

Michael *JORDAN*

GUARD - CHICAGO BULLS (1984—1993, 1995—1998)

Jordan doesn't make just the Mount Rushmore of Chicago sports. He makes the Mount Rushmore of North American sports. He makes the Mount Rushmore of world sports. Not only was Jordan the most hyped athlete of all time; he lived up to the hype and pressure like no other athlete before or since.

"He just made you wish that for one day that you could fly in the air," former rival Magic Johnson said. "You wonder what it would be like."

We've all wondered what it would be like to be Jordan. He was just a skinny 19-year-old freshman at North Carolina who had the guts to take and make a national championship-winning shot. He blossomed into the best player in the country, the best player on a loaded 1984 US Olympic team that won the gold medal, the No. 3 overall pick by the Bulls in 1984, and an instant NBA phenomenon.

Then the endorsements rolled in. Nike, McDonald's, Gatorade, Chevrolet, and others wanted to be part of the Jordan brand. Soon, Jordan wasn't just a Chicago or American star but a worldwide celebrity. And while his name was exploding off the court, we all watched him struggle on the court to become a champion and fulfill his destiny.

Though he was brilliant, the suffering he experienced at the hands of the Pistons humanized him to us. We saw Jordan limp off the court in defeat in 1988, 1989, and 1990 against the mean and rugged Pistons and realized that even Jordan, the greatest player of them all, had challenges that he needed time to overcome. That just made us rejoice when he finally reached the mountaintop in 1991.

There are so many moments that make Jordan what he is and illustrate his meaning: He was the star of the Dream Team. He didn't stop at just one, two, or three titles. His game evolved from the high-flying act to one that was more cerebral but just as deadly. Most important, his desire to win never waned.

Never once was he satisfied. He expected perfection of his teammates and himself. Fittingly, Jordan's last shot with the Bulls was a perfect 18-footer that swished perfectly through a net in Utah. The form was perfect, the release was perfect, and the result was the perfectly appropriate sixth championship.

Now, as Jordan's career fades further and further into history, his legacy grows bigger and bigger. Basketball players all over the world still wear Air Jordan shoes. The Jordan Brand, an offshoot of Nike, is the official outfitter of multiple college athletics programs and one of the most sought-after suppliers. *Space Jam*, the campy 1996 live-action cartoon, grossed more than $230 million at the box office when it was first released and is still a hit for fans who remember Jordan's playing career and even those who don't.

"In the years since this 90-minute product placement was unleashed, it's taken on a significance within the culture that might not be appropriate for a film where Porky Pig wets himself," *The Guardian* wrote. "Some have begged for the long-rumored sequel starring LeBron James to finally come to fruition. Others, such as the NBA player Patrick Patterson, have claimed that *Space Jam* is 'the perfect movie' and is too sacred to ever replicate."

Whatever. But Jordan's career is too sacred to replicate.

Every great young player is compared with Jordan in some way or another. Ask Kobe Bryant about that. Ask LeBron James about that. They've heard the comparisons and fought against them, but one thing is always true:

There will never be another Jordan. Nobody will ever come close.

Walter *PAYTON*

RUNNING BACK - CHICAGO BEARS (1975–1987)

Payton simply kept going and going and going. His legs never stopped churning, his arms were always ready for the next battle, his lungs and heart working like machines. Payton was the ultimate athlete and competitor who welcomed all physical and mental challenges.

Even the one challenge he couldn't beat—bile duct cancer—was one that Payton fought with his typical determination before dying in 1999 at age 45. It was also a wakeup call that if the unstoppable Payton could die in his 40s, anybody could go at any time.

"Walter didn't care about how important he was. He lived 45 years, and he touched more people than we know," teammate Revie Sorey said. "Walter has given us the best wakeup call ever. He died with his toughness, so he is making us tough. The benchmark was raised a couple of notches when God made Walter."

Whoever made Payton made a once-in-a-generation athlete who persisted until finally reaching his ultimate goal.

Drafted fourth overall out of Jackson State, a historically black college in Mississippi, Payton made an immediate impact in 1975. After the early retirements of Gale Sayers and Dick Butkus and still seven years before the hiring of Mike Ditka, the Bears needed an identity. Payton provided that, barreling headfirst into opponents and never shying away from contact.

Payton eventually set the NFL record for yards in a game and a career (both since broken) as he kept the Bears competitive until the rest of the roster caught up. The first record to fall was the mark for yards in a game, when he ran for 275 against Minnesota on a dreary November day in 1977, breaking O.J. Simpson's mark of 273. Ailing with the flu, Payton willed the Bears to a 10–7 win that helped them eventually get to the playoffs for the first time in 14 years.

"Maybe it'll mean something later, in three or four years when I'm out, but right now it's just another game," Payton said then.

On October 7, 1984, he became the NFL's all-time leading rusher when he picked up 6 yards on a toss play during a win over New Orleans. True to form, Payton had asked the Bears to keep any celebrations short.

"I didn't want to stop the game and stop our momentum," he said. "The thing I was thinking about most was getting the photographers off the field and to start playing again so maybe we could get a quick score. We didn't have enough points. I wanted to get everybody off the field so we could score some more."

By then, the Bears had built a team worthy of Payton.

They went 10–6 in 1984 and lost the NFC Championship Game to the 49ers. In 1985, the 31-year-old Payton rushed for 1,551 yards as the Bears went 15–1 on their way to winning Super Bowl XX.

"You don't say Payton's a leader," Dan Hampton said in 1985. "Payton's beyond a leader. It's hard to put into words what he does for this team. He's irreplaceable. It's going to be a sad day when he leaves Chicago."

Payton retired after the 1987 season and became a staple of Chicago. His death in 1999 was shocking, but his influence and legacy will never wane.

"On this Soldier Field and dozens more, he was a football warrior and gladiator," then-NFL commissioner Paul Tagliabue said during a memorial service for Payton. "In the eyes of many, he was the greatest football player of all time."

INDEX

ABOUT THE AUTHOR

Brian Sandalow is a freelance sports reporter in Chicago who has written extensively for the *Chicago Sun-Times*, the Associated Press, the Sports Xchange, and ChicagoSide Sports. Raised in suburban Skokie and a graduate of the University of Missouri, Brian has covered just about everything in Chicago sports, ranging from the Cubs to New Zealand rugby, the Blackhawks to international soccer, and pretty much anything in between.

ACKNOWLEDGMENTS

I would like to thank my parents, Eileen and Barry, for pushing me to pursue my goals and indulging my love of sports. My brother Scott has always challenged my ideas and competed with me, forcing me to think bigger and more creatively.

My wife, Jennifer, has had to put up with my late nights at numerous ballparks and arenas, and done so with nothing but love.

Finally, I would not have written this book if not for editors at the *Sun-Times*, Associated Press, and ChicagoSide who decided to take a chance on me and publish my work.